The ENCORE Approach for Financial Advisors

Delivering the Ultimate Client Experience

Less Stress, More Income, Greater Personal Freedom

Written by:

Rob Brown

Founder

Encore Partners

www.encorepartners.com

Copyright Information

About Encore Partners

Encore Partners is a client-driven training and consulting firm that helps grow the businesses of financial service companies and their advisors. We use a combination of personal and Web-based solutions to help individuals and organizations achieve greater productivity and higher levels of personal and professional satisfaction. Our consultation, training courses, and speaking engagements are supported by our Website, EncorePartners.com.

From showing you how to clearly articulate your value to building your team, our techniques enable you to capitalize on existing client relationships and rapidly build new ones. We call this "Creating Encores," a disciplined, six-step approach to practice management. Through coaching and training programs, we are committed to strengthening your practice and increasing your success.

Learn More…free videos and downloads

If you would like to learn even more about the topics presented in this book, please visit the Encore Library, www.EncorePartners.com/UCEbook. You'll find many helpful downloads and videos for putting these Ultimate Client Experience concepts to work right away.

Hello, my name is Rob Brown.

 I'm committed to helping you build happier client relationships, more freedom and greater profits. During my 29-year career, I've been a successful producer and valued mentor. My background also includes executive management with a full-service financial services firm. My responsibilities have always focused on **helping advisors grow their practices through coaching, training, fee-based initiatives, technology enhancements, and wealth management.**

I've defined all of my roles with the belief that the advisor is the ultimate determinate of success of any financial services organization. Find ways to make the advisor more effective in building and maintaining client relationships and **the client, firm, and advisor will all benefit.**

Through my Website, www.EncorePartners.com, and personal coaching engagements, I've worked with hundreds advisors from dozens of broker-dealers and investment advisory firms and through their strategic partnerships. These relationships include UBS, Wells Fargo Advisors, Schwab Advisor Services, Century Securities, Commonwealth Securities, H.D. Vest, John Hancock, Merrill Lynch, MFS, Morgan Stanley, Scott & Stringfellow, Securities America, Sentinel Investments, and Sterne Agee.

I've been a speaker at Securities Industry and Financial Market Association (SIFMA) and American Banker Association (ABA) events. Early in my career, I was a regular financial columnist for the *Richmond Times-Dispatch* and a contributing author to

Horsesmouth.com. I've been quoted in *On Wall Street* and *Information Week* magazines.

I'm a graduate of Randolph-Macon College with a degree in economics and business. I also completed the prestigious Securities Industry Institute program at the Wharton School of Business of the University of Pennsylvania.

I've been married for 28 years. My wife, Lori, and I are blessed with triplet daughters who are all college graduates.

Our clients are achieving encores...

"Rob Brown's approach to the 'Ultimate Client Experience' is a road map that takes the reader to the promised land of how we should all be running our business and serving our clients. By working with Rob, I've moved my business from one with satisfied clients and limited referrals to one where my only problem is keeping up with the growth."

—Ron Dickinson, CPA, CFP®, MPA-Tax
Dickinson Investment Advisors

"The 'Ultimate Client' concept has had a profound impact on our firm. By clearly defining the way we deliver service, our clients have become more loyal and they have entrusted us with even more of their assets. If you put Rob Brown's strategies into action, you win, your team wins, and, most important, your clients win."

—Michael Lutz, CFP®, CEO
Legacy Financial Strategies

"Rob's advice isn't theoretical – it's practical. He doesn't just talk about the 'why,' he talks about the 'what' and the 'how,' based on real-world, proven techniques. The advisors in our organization who have chosen to follow Rob's advice are now delivering consistent service, getting more referrals, and spending less on client acquisition, building more efficient and successful teams that are poised to grow substantially."

—Dee Costa, President
Asset Marketing Systems

"*Delivering the Ultimate Client Experience* is excellent reading for all advisors – from top producers to the novice. Rob shows you step-by-step how to provide the Ultimate Client Experience to your clients and prospects, so they will stand up and take notice. You will differentiate yourself from other advisors and grow your business."

—**Peter Lantos, Founder**
The Elite Advisor

"Rob's common-sense approach to delivering client service is refreshing. No outlandish, high cost tactics – he keeps it simple and makes it actionable. I would not be at the level I am without his diligent approach and expertise!"

—**Patrick Bykerk**
Financial Consultant, Branch Manager
Raymond James

Table of Contents

Welcome!

Welcome and congratulations!

Your commitment to the E.N.C.O.R.E. approach to practice management is an invaluable step toward happier clients, more freedom, and greater profits. In this book, we'll focus on the Navigate – the second stage in our six-step E.N.C.O.R.E. approach. This book utilizes unique information design principles to ensure that you climb quickly up the learning curve. Upon completion of this book and absorption of the principles we outline here, you may wish to move on to subsequent modules. More information about additional modules can be obtained by visiting our Website at www.EncorePartners.com.

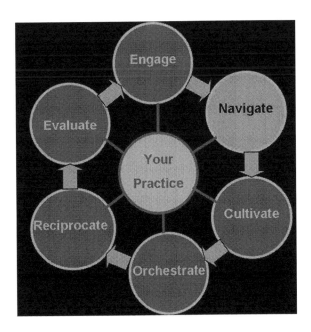

Thanks for purchasing this book

I know you'll be able to use this straightforward approach to re-energize your business and move to your highest level of success! To get even more out of this book, visit www.EncorePartners.com/UCEbook. You'll find additional free resources, including downloads and videos, for putting the Ultimate Client Experience ideas to work right away. If you have any questions, please send me an email, at Robb@EncorePartners.com. I wish you the very best in creating encores – a key to success in both business and in life.

Chapter 1:

Delivering the Ultimate Client Experience

Often, the day-to-day challenges of running your business keep you from spending time where it matters most – working with your clients. Yet, the more time you spend with your clients, the better the job you will do for them, and the more your business will grow. This Chapter walks you through six stages for "Delivering the Ultimate Client Experience" which will help you jump-start your production and take your practice to new levels of success.

Your clients should view you as an indispensable resource – a trusted advisor worthy of increased referrals and new business opportunities. What's more, when you exceed your clients' expectations, your business will flourish.

Introduction

> *"The sure way to miss success is to miss the opportunity."*
> —*Victor Chasles*

Providing superior client service is perhaps the greatest missed opportunity among financial advisors today. Stop for a moment and consider these statements:

- Your clients are your greatest asset
- When you build client loyalty and confidence, you capture new business and high quality referrals
- Providing superior client service and advice means your work is more satisfying and rewarding
- The more time you spend in client-facing activities, the more income you will generate for your practice and yourself
- Your client service model makes client-acquisition easier; your prospects know how they will be treated when they become clients of your practice

To some, these phrases state the obvious. After all, top advisors leverage these concepts every day; they work hard to spend as much time with their clients as possible. Unfortunately, most advisors spend less than half their time in client-facing activities. What's more, the majority of financial advisors lack a client communication plan – a simple calendar for scheduling and tracking basic contacts.

Sure, there are many seemingly reasonable excuses for this lack of client attention. From poor organizational skills to a shortage of time to lack of financial resources, the list appears endless. Yet, this one area of practice management separates many high achievement advisors from the rest.

When you have a good system, gathering new assets and referrals from your current clients can be simple. When you deliver a high level of service, your clients will:

- Add to their existing holdings
- Buy new products and services
- Give you high-quality referrals

We're going to provide you with that system in this book. The results will be astounding.

Before you get started, let's consider one important question.

Do You REALLY Want "Ideal" Clients?

Be honest.

Does all the talk you hear about the "ideal client" make you want to throw up?

In reality, it's become gibberish.

From recruiting messages to pitches from would-be coaches to fodder that fills the pages of the industry rags; it's a be-all and end-all solution for developing your *ideal business*. I've used the term myself…a few million times.

But now it rings hollow.

Sure, it sounds great…until you put it into practice.

As hard as you might try, you tell yourself you'll never have a book full of ideal clients. The pretenders and wannabes seem to slip through the cracks.

- They have a lot of money. But they don't do a lot of business.
- They do a lot of business. But they are jerks.
- They're really, really nice. But they don't take your advice.

- They take your advice readily. But, they're constantly pestering you.

And the beat goes on.

So you end up working with *mostly* ideal clients, figuring the rest are just the price you pay for being in the business. A little penance on earth…a *NOT*-so-ideal business, after all.

Have I struck a nerve?

Good.

Now, let me dig a little deeper. I don't want to let you off the hook. No excuse-making.

Ideal is not good enough.

Eliminating marginal clients is easy.

To build a practice that will truly make you proud…a business with sustainable long-term economic value…you need to seek out your *ultimate clients*.

Ultimate clients are *more* than ideal. They add purpose to your business and life. They make everything you do more enjoyable. They don't keep you a secret.

You end up with the *ultimate business*.

Want proof?

Take a close look at your list of ideal clients. They're probably the ones generating 80% or more of your revenues. Or, they represent 80% or more of the assets you manage.

And, if the 80/20 rule holds true…they represent about 20% of your clients. Most of the 7-figure producers I coach see these numbers play out closer to 90/10. They get 90% of their production from 10% of their clients.

Don't stop here…let's go deeper.

Now, handpick the top 20% of that list…the top 20% of your top 10 or 20%. This time, don't just go by raw production and asset numbers. Add some qualitative aspects as to why they make the grade.

Here are some questions you might ask yourself…

- Do you *really* like them?
- Do they like you?
- Do they send you referrals?
- Do they treat your teammates well?
- Do they quickly accept your advice?
- Do they fit into a niche you enjoy?

Go ahead and add your own questions. These are *your* favorite clients. If you had to start your business all over again, these folks would be the first ones you'd pick.

For most financial advisors, this new list numbers fewer than 20. And these very special clients represent about 64% of your business. That's 80% of the 80% with which you began this exercise.

The 80/20 rule is an endless loop.

Now, stop for a few minutes. Really think about the way your business would feel if it was filled with these ultimate clients. The best of *your* best.

What if your ultimate clients made up 100% of your business…not just 64%?

It would be more – much more – than just ideal. You would have your ultimate business. If you get serious, it's not just a pipedream.

Are you worth it?

During a fairly recent coaching assignment, I worked with an advisor who did just north of $1,200,000 in business with 212 households. On the first pass, he found that 87% of his fees came from 17% of his clients. That's $1,044,000 from 36 clients.

In other words, 176 clients represented 13% of his business…a real eye-opener all by itself. Think of all the time his team had to spend on this really small percentage of his revenues.

But we didn't stop there.

I asked him to handpick his top eight clients. Which clients would he keep, if he could *only* keep 20% of his top 36 clients? He used questions like the ones I listed above.

When he was done, he was surprised that a few *big* clients didn't make the grade. He didn't enjoy working with them.

Even so, when we did the math, these eight clients represented 61% of his total production. He was getting $732,000 in business from just eight clients. 4% of his clients were generating 61% of his business.

And…drum roll please…these are the clients he enjoys the most. These are *not* just his ideal clients, they're his *Ultimate Clients*. The bedrock of his business.

The implications for this advisors' business are mind-blowing.

It starts, simply enough, with client acquisition.

By attracting just six more ultimate clients, he could eliminate 204 other clients and still do the same amount of production. Adding eight ultimate clients would increase his business by over 20%.

The benefits would compound.

He would have more time and fewer headaches. He would have more than an ideal business…he would have his *ultimate* business.

That's powerful information for deciding the type of business *you* would like to have.

For determining who you accept as new clients, for building the long-term economic value of your business, and for spending your time on the stuff that matters most to you, "ideal clients" is no longer good enough. It's a catchphrase.

By focusing your business around your *ultimate* clients you can have your *ultimate* business.

Take some time to run these numbers on your practice. They'll give you a great backdrop for the rest of this book. Plus, you'll be even better prepared to create the Ultimate Client Service Model.

What is Client Service?

Before we can talk about delivering the ultimate client experience, we need to be sure we have a clear definition of client service. There are many definitions but, for our purposes, during this Chapter, I use "client service" to mean "personal attention and communication." In his book, *The Only Thing That Matters*, Karl Albrecht said, "Client service is being attentive to the *person* behind the need, and responding to the person more than just responding to the need."

When you think about client service and, in particular, when you think about delivering the ultimate client experience, remember you're talking about how you interact with your clients and not the process that you take them through. Your clients are not their financial plan; your clients are not their money. They are people, and you need to give them personal, one-on-one attention.

To do this, you need to communicate well. They need to understand who you are, what you do, why you do what you do, and how you'll help them achieve their goals. Ralph Waldo Emerson said, "It is a luxury to be understood." This is particularly true for delivering the ultimate client experience; make sure your clients clearly understand what you do.

Why is Client Service Important? Some Studies

To bear this point out, let's answer the question, "Why is client service important?" Let's look specifically at a few excerpts from studies that have been conducted in the financial services industry over the past couple years.

"The **fastest-growing registered investment advisors** in 2012 saw net organic growth rise five times faster than all other firms because they excel at delivering 'the client experience' and as a result get more referrals." —Schwab Advisor Services Benchmarking Survey, ThinkAdvisor.com, 2013

"**67% of advisors** say they have a 'personal relationship' with their clients. **Only 38% of clients** reported the same." — Accenture, "Closing the Gap: How Tech-Savvy Advisors Can Regain Investor Trust, 2013"

"Communication is crucial to investor satisfaction. The highest ratings come from investors contacted 12 or more times a year…The study finds that communicating the right information and using the delivery channels investors prefer at the optimal frequency improves overall investor satisfaction, which is likely to yield clear financial benefits for investment firms." —J.D. Power & Associates, *U.S. Full Service Investor Satisfaction Study, 2013.*

We have seen similar results in hundreds of studies going as far back as we can we remember. This is what we help you deal with in *Delivering the Ultimate Client Experience.* This Chapter walks you through the six stages for taking your client-service model to the next level:

1. Define your client segments
2. Clarify your client-management process
3. Build an ongoing client communication calendar
4. Monitor your time each day
5. Turn your clients into advocates of your practice

6. Be spontaneous – offer something special

When you deliver the ultimate client experience, you increase client satisfaction, reduce your stress, and generate a steady stream of referrals. This decreases your dependency on expensive, time-consuming prospecting and you'll still have more income. These are all positives, so let's get into each of these steps, one at a time.

Stage 1: Define Your Client Segments

Unless you work exclusively with a highly scrutinized clientele, segmenting or re-segmenting your clients is an important first step to delivering the ultimate client experience. Not all clients want, need, or deserve the same level of attention. Develop your service model to cater to the needs of your top clients and those who have the potential to be top clients....your *ultimate* clients.

Defining your client segments is the first stage of delivering the ultimate client experience and is as simple as A, B, C – putting your clients into A, B, C or 1, 2, 3 groupings.

To get started, make sure you have a definition of an ultimate client for your business – *not* somebody else's definition, but *your* definition! It may be based on net worth, on commissions paid, on fees generated, on referrals given, on how easy they are to deal with, or a combination of any of these things. Those ultimate clients – people who meet the criteria you've set for your practice – are your "A" clients and they deserve the ultimate client experience.

This is not to say you'll treat "B" or "C" clients poorly, but they haven't yet earned the right to receive – and probably don't want – the same level of service as your "A" clients.

Your "B" clients are that middle group; they may meet two or three out of your four criteria for an ultimate client relationship. You aren't sure yet if they'll become "A" clients, but they may – if they can overcome those one or two criteria they haven't yet accomplished. You need to position those clients through profiling, to determine if they can become "A" clients. Perhaps you deliver almost all of the "A" level services, letting them know they're not quite getting it all.

Finally, your "C" clients: the big question with your "C" clients is, "To keep or not to keep?" Some advisors don't like to give up any clients at all. They're afraid, as soon as they give them up, client will win the lottery or bring in a big inheritance. I would suggest, if you're not currently delivering some level of consistent service to those clients when they *do* win the lottery or receive a big inheritance, they won't call you anyway. They don't know you want their business! You haven't earned it. Why would a "C" client give you a lot of money when they didn't hear from you before, when they had a little bit of money? You need to decide, instead, whether or not to keep your "C" clients and, if you do decide to keep them, you need to deliver a consistent level of service that will keep you on their radar screen if they *do* manage to win the lottery. By keeping "C" clients, you're saying you have some expectation – albeit long-term – that, one day, they'll move up your client segment scale. If this isn't the case, you'll be better off if you can find another advisor to handle their needs.

The key action point here is to define those segments.

- Define your ultimate clients – your "A" clients.

- Those among your existing clientele who, over the next six to twelve months, have the potential to become "A" clients, but aren't there yet, are your "B" clients.

- All the others are "C" clients who still get some consistent service, if you're going to keep them, but not the same level of service as your "B" clients or your "A" clients.

To help you through this process of defining your client segments, look at your current definition of an ideal client and update and refine it. Or better yet, set your sights on ultimate clients. If you don't have your definition down yet, you should establish one now.

Finally, make sure, once you've segmented your clients, you note those classifications in your contact management system so you can keep up with them in a way that's commensurate with the service schedule you'll define.

Stage 2: Clarify Your Client-Management Process (CMP)

Your CMP is the primary strategy you utilize to manage and monitor the financial side of your client relationships. It could be comprehensive financial planning, asset allocation, estate preservation, retirement income planning, or any of a number of other specialties. Delivering the ultimate client experience requires that your process be well-defined and delivered consistently. Though you may choose to offer or outsource related services, your professionalism and expertise are best evidenced by the way you implement your Client-Management Process.

How do you work all of your clients through a process of bringing them into your practice, servicing them on a regular basis, *and* earning referrals? It needs to be consistent, no matter what type of business you're in. You could be an RIA, a fee-based advisor, a stockbroker, a financial planner, an insurance specialist, or a wealth manger – you need to have a very clearly-defined client-management process.

Another way to think about this process is to ask yourself a few questions:

- How do your clients do business with you? If I were to introduce you to a brand new prospect, how would you describe the way in which they would become a client of your practice, and how would you manage that relationship and service that relationship over time?

- What is your "core" process? Are you an asset allocator, are you an estate planner, are you an investment manager, do you perform comprehensive financial planning or wealth management?

- Your client-management process: is it consistent, is it well-articulated, is it consultative? When you describe it to someone you're meeting for the first time, do they truly understand how you do business? Are they then willing to give you information and not quiz you a whole lot about how you're going to implement those plans – because they already understand the process?

All client-management processes have five basic steps. You start by being able to describe your story and your process in a presentation. You then gather or update profiles and objectives by having a consistent questionnaire. You then develop and deliver proposals and recommendations. You do this through financial planning or an investment management process and you follow it up on a regular basis through monitor and review. That's a brief, somewhat generic definition of a client-management process. What's your process? Is it clear? Do you really know what it is? Do you deliver it the same way with each client and prospect each time, whether you're working with a big client or someone you don't know quite so well, who may become a top client of your practice?

Your client-management process is really a never-ending process and needs to be tweaked all the time. However, it should be consistent and you need to be able to articulate it clearly. Can you do that? You need to be able to meet this requirement, to deliver the ultimate client experience.

Stage 3: Build a Communication Calendar

At a minimum, your top clients expect and deserve 24 touches each year. These contacts are at the heart of delivering the ultimate client experience. Your touches could include letters, emails, calls, meetings, Webinars, Website and social media posts and special events. Some of these contacts need to be highly customized while others may be less personal. Although you may think you make 24 contacts to each of your best clients during the course of a typical year, you shouldn't leave it to chance. Build your foundation for superior client service by designing a communication calendar that outlines your touches for the year ahead – or at least for the next quarter.

At the heart of delivering the ultimate client experience is stage three, building a communication calendar. Notice the word "communication." Communication, as I explained earlier, is central to good client service and to delivering the ultimate client experience. You need to have a calendar that allows you to clearly deliver communication on a regular basis. This calendar should enable you to deliver those 24 contacts in a year. It should also allow you to spend more than two thirds of your time in client-facing activities.

To start, you need some tools. You have calls, you have meetings, and you have letters, emails, workshops, and special events. You plug these tools into your calendar. Then, you need to vary your message style. You can't come across as being sterile. Your style has to denote *personal* attention, so you need to have very personal communications, you need to have targeted communications, and you need to have general communications. Some of these communications will be generated internally and others will be generated externally.

Once you know what your tools are, you need to decide how you want to deliver those tools and vary the style, so it comes across as being personal. Then, you need to execute with consistency by planning a little bit in advance – which can be difficult for a lot of financial advisors. The best way to get started is make sure you have at least the next three months of your communication calendar built out. Then, each month, you add a month to the end of that calendar, so your calendar is always at least three months ahead. This allows you to update, to revise, to fine-tune, and to do a better job of delivering communication through your calendar, ultimately delivering the client experience you want your "A" clients to have.

Earlier, I mentioned you need to vary your message. I talked about personal, general, and targeted communication. Personal is somewhat obvious – this is the phone calls you make, the in-person meetings you have, the personal notes or emails you write. However, not everything you do – even with your best clients – can be personal to that level, so you need to build in some general communication. These could be communications that you send to all your client segments – "A," "B," and "C." They're not customized; they have more universal themes. They're perhaps general letters or newsletters. They're things you put on your Website. They could be research, investment digests, an economic outlook, or financial-planning concepts. Perhaps, once a quarter, you send a general newsletter to all your "A" and "B" clients and do that twice a year for "C" clients. That's the first way to vary your message with general communication.

The second way is through targeted communication. Some of these border on personal; in fact, personal communications are really a group or subset of targeted communications. Perhaps you have some of your "A" clients who have an interest in a particular type of investment, or you're doing a particular type of planning for them – estate planning or philanthropic planning, for example. They could receive a more targeted communication on those topics that wouldn't be included in the general communication in the other category. Targeted communication could also include some personal notes, telephone calls, and in-person meetings. It could be a "call me" communication – maybe sending out a copy of a statement or an updated plan that you've done for them, with a note that says, "Call me at your convenience; I'd like to go over this." It tells them you're thinking about them and that they can just call you when they're ready, but it's not urgent – that's why you're not calling. It could be specific information about an account – maybe a circled statement, saying, "Call me urgently – we need to talk about this specific investment!" It could be targeted promotions about a specific product or service you'd like to cross-sell. This could be a phone call, mail, or an email.

You can conduct luncheons, workshops, or appreciation events and, depending upon the scale of those events, you can invite certain types of clients. Perhaps you have an over-all client event once a year, inviting all your clients across segments. But, once a month, you hold a luncheon for 10 of your "A" clients. There are a lot of different ways to do this but, in building your communication calendar (we'll go into more detail on this soon), think about those general communications and think about those targeted communications – both at a high level and at a very personal level. Build out the number of contacts you want to make with your clients on an annual basis.

Segment	Targeted	General	Medium	What
A	12-4-4	6	Call Meeting Mail/Email	Wealth Mgt Research/ Topical
B	6-3-0	8	Call Meetings Mail/Email	Research/ Topical
C	3-0-0	10	Call Mail/Email	Research
Connections / Best Prospects	6-2-0	6	Call Meeting Mail/Email	Topical

A table like the one above will help you determine the number – not when, but the number – of contacts you might make to your different client segments.

The **Segment** column describes your different client segments – "A," "B," or "C" – so you have one row per segment. You can add a row for your connections or your best prospects.

The second column – **Targeted** – specifies how many targeted communications each segment will get. In this example, the "A" clients will receive twenty targeted communications during the course of the year, the "B" clients will receive nine, the "C" group three, and good connections – or your best prospects – might receive eight. The hyphenated format allows you to further specify how many phone calls, meetings, and personalized notes you are allotting to each segment. For example, in the above table, we're allotting twelve phone calls, four in-person meetings, and four personalized emails for each of our "A" clients.

The next column – **General** – describes the number of general communications your various client segments and connections will receive during the year.

The **Medium** column specifies the form in which those communications are delivered. For your "A" clients, the 12-4-4 targeted communications that are listed first could be:

- One telephone call a month – a total of twelve phone calls over the year,
- Four review meetings in a year, and
- Four personal emails that you send them a year.

That's how you'd get in 20 targeted contacts a year to your "A" clients. Add 6 general contacts through the mail and your "A" clients already have 26 contacts!

January	July
Themes: New Year, Martin Luther King Day	**Themes:** Independence Day (US), Canada Day
Encore Library: • Simple New Year Letter and Profiling Exercise	**Encore Library:** • 9 Steps for Using Email in Your Ongoing Client Communications
Possible Focus: General Financial Planning, Prior Year Goal Review, Wealth Management	**Possible Focus:** Risk Management, Asset Allocation
February	August
Themes: Presidents' Day, Family Day (Canada)	**Themes:** End of Vacation Season
Encore Library: • Tax Planning Letter and Tip Sheet	**Encore Library:** • 6 Good Reasons to Call Your Clients NOW
Possible Focus: Asset Allocation, Life Insurance	**Possible Focus:** Alternative Investments

March	September
Themes: St Patrick's Day, DST begins, Easter	**Themes:** Labor Day, Jewish New Year, Back to School
Encore Library: • Client Appreciation Letter • Daylight Saving Time Client Letter	**Encore Library:** • Client Advocacy and Referrals
Possible Focus: Retirement Planning, IRA Rollovers	**Possible Focus:** College Planning and Financial Aid
April	October
Themes: April 15th Tax and IRA Deadline, Jewish Passover	**Themes:** Halloween, Columbus Day, Thanksgiving (Canada), Yom Kippur, DST ends
Encore Library: • Helping Your Clients Avoid Costly Mistakes	**Encore Library:** • Year End Tax Planning Campaign for Clients and Prospects
Possible Focus: Tax Favored Investing, 401(k) Investment Choices	**Possible Focus:** Charitable Giving, Family Gifting

May	November
Themes: Memorial Day, Victoria Day, Mother's Day, Cinco de Mayo	**Themes:** Election Day, Thanksgiving (US), Veterans Day, Remembrance Day
Encore Library: • Add to Your Clients' Summer Reading List	**Encore Library:** • A Time to Say Thanks
Possible Focus: Estate Planning, Wealth Management	**Possible Focus:** General Financial Planning, Wealth Management
June	December
Themes: Summer, Father's Day	**Themes:** Christmas, Hanukkah, Boxing Day
Encore Library: • 3 Client Letters – Saying Thank You Builds Lifelong Relationships	**Encore Library:** • How to Easily Build Handwritten Notes into Your Ongoing Client Care Routines
Possible Focus: Long Term Care, Health and Disability Insurance	**Possible Focus:** Asset Allocation, Tax Planning, Goal Setting

Once you know the number of contacts you're going to deliver to each group, you need to develop themes around those contacts, to make it easier to deliver them. We would recommend having a theme for each month. The table above gives you some ideas about what those themes could include. For example, in January, you may want to deliver a "look-back" or a "look-forward" letter; you can find an example of these in the Encore Library (www.EncorePartners.com/UCEbook). In February, you may want to help your clients get their tax information together, so you may send a letter, along with tax forms. Maybe, for fun – if you have an Irish background, or you know clients who have an Irish background – you send out St. Patrick's Day cards. In the summer, you can send out a nice letter talking about Independence Day and the great country that we live in. So, first, decide on the number of contacts per segment then begin building a theme-based calendar to round those contacts out.

There are also a good number of tools in the Encore Library (www.EncorePartners.com/UCEbook). They will help you build the communication calendar.

Complete the four-step process:

1. Decide on the number of contacts you want to make with each group each year.
2. Realistically establish your message styles. Don't say you're going to make 28 personal contacts to each one of your 150 best clients – you'll never be able to do it. Make it realistic!
3. Next, build a calendar around that information.
4. Finally, start gathering your resources – what you'll send your clients. Put a big file in your desk drawer into which you throw brochures, letters, things you see from competitors or

strategic partners that you can imitate or adapt to your communication calendar.

Stage 4: Monitor Your Time Each Day

> Advisors who spend more than 50% of their time in client-facing activities have happier clients and higher incomes than those who spend less. To deliver the ultimate client experience, you should color-code your calendar, to monitor the amount of time you're dedicating and spending with clients and prospects. Most electronic calendars, such as Outlook, give you this option. If you use a paper-based calendar, use different color pens or highlighters. This simple technique will help you budget your time going forward and measure your results as you look back.

The fourth stage of developing the ultimate client experience is monitoring your time each day. Before I talk more specifically about what you should be doing with your time each day, let me reiterate a key concept. Advisors who spend more than half of their time in client-facing activities have incomes that are two to three times greater than those who don't. Time is money. Especially when it comes to time spent with current and future clients.

In my experience coaching advisors, taking formal and informal polls during training programs, and conducting online surveys, most advisors are in the 25%-to-40% range, so they're at the low end of a satisfactory level of income. Sure, there are exceptions but, when you consider the direct correlation between how much time you spend in client-facing activities and your income, it seems to me that's an extremely important focus point for your day.

While you're thinking about your day, it's important to have goals. It's important to know what you're working towards... *but...* it's even *more* important to think about activities. What activities are important to you in the way that you run your practice?

When I was actively involved in my advisory practice, I had a simple rule for my business; it helped me triple my production: *12 by 12; 2 by 5; plan each day*. I knew that, if I talked to 12 clients or prospects before noon each day (12 by 12), met with 10 clients or prospects each week (2 by 5), and spent time at the end of each day planning for the following day, the rest of my business results would take care of themselves. I had my client-facing activities covered. I knew what I was doing, from a phone-calling perspective, to clients and future clients, active prospects, and inactive prospects. I knew how many appointments I needed to have each week, to be able to work through gathering data, making presentations and reviewing clients' portfolios. I knew what I needed to do, from a networking connections perspective.

Of course, there are other activities that aren't included in the *12 by 12, 2 by 5 and plan each day*, such as meeting time, service time, and planning time. But, once I was able to align my day around the *12 by 12; 2 by 5; plan each day* principle, I could fit those other pieces in and it was much easier to build my schedule. One of the things we really want you to do as you work through this process of monitoring your time is to take a look back and measure the kinds of activities you're putting in today. Set a standard – a goal for where you'd like to be – then build an ideal day.

I was talking with an advisor with whom I'm doing some coaching work and she told me that, just by adopting the *12 by 12; 2 by 5; plan each day,* she did more business in eight weeks than she'd done in the previous three months put together. A simple idea applied to her way of doing business made a significant jump in her business. Test it yourself. Build your calendar around your client-facing activities. Maybe your numbers won't be *exactly* the same as mine, but they'll probably be somewhat similar, based on the way you do business.

Stage 5: Turn Your Clients into Advocates

Advocacy is a process for turning your clients into promoters of your business. Advocacy leads to new business and asset opportunities, as well as highly qualified referrals and references. When advocacy is communicated properly and frequently, your clients see it as a mutually beneficial and highly professional attribute of your business. To deliver the ultimate client experience, you need to make sure advocacy is part of your client service offerings. As the year gets underway, build advocacy discussions into your review meetings and continue with this dialog throughout the year.

Referrals are an important part of any successful advisor's practice. Our primary method for helping our advisor clients build more referrals is to help them turn their clients into advocates. An advocate is a person or group of people who have an almost inexplicable desire to see you and your practice succeed. They are promoters, they are campaigners, and they are supporters. When your clients are advocates, you'll get a steady flow of high-quality referrals – referrals that look like your current ideal clients.

Let me give an example from my career. I have a great client who lives a couple of hours from my hometown of Williamsburg,

Virginia. Once or twice a year, he calls me and asks me to play golf in a very beautiful part of the state. Of course, I don't mind being invited to play golf, but what's better is this client has trained himself – actually, *he* probably taught *me* a lot about advocacy. Each time I play golf with him, he fills out the foursome with two other people who are friends of his he believes will be good clients for my practice. He's truly a promoter, a supporter of my business. He knows that, by giving me these referrals and references, my job is easier – and, when my job is easier, I can do a better job for him. Advocacy is mutually beneficial.

Advocacy is a process of understanding who your clients are, what you know about them, what clubs they belong to, what activities they're involved in, who they know, and who you can uncover that they know through your knowledge of those events and activities in which they're involved.

You should be able to specifically suggest to your clients the names of people you've run across when researching clubs they belong to. When you suggest to them that person may be a good client of your practice and ask them for their opinion, they'll give you high-quality referrals – there's no doubt about it. They may be referrals to those specific people you referenced, but they may also be referrals to other people they may know. After your clients know the kind of person you're looking for as a new client, they may provide referrals that fit better into your practice. By not leaving it open-ended, it makes it easier for your client to give you a reference, because they know specifically what you're asking for. Don't say, "Oh, you know, if maybe you could give me a referral to somebody" and hand over your card – that's a very uncomfortable sort of referral request. Instead, specifically say something like, "You know, Rob, I ran across

Joe's name in the listing of members of your club. Do you know Joe? Do you think he would be a good client of my practice?"

This kind of approach makes it easier for your client to give you a referral, because they know specifically what you're asking for! Besides, when you do this, your client feels rewarded – they appreciate the fact that you care about their opinion. They know that, the more they help you, the better the job you can do for them.

Turning your clients into advocates may *seem* like it goes outside of actually building your ultimate client experience. As a matter of fact, it's actually *additive* to your ultimate client experience because you're not just able to spend more time with people who are just like your ultimate clients, you're also able to cut down on your prospecting time.

That's it for stage five. If you're trying to build the ultimate client experience, you need to turn your clients into advocates of your practice. It's good for you and it's good for them.

Stage 6: Be Spontaneous – Offer Something Special

Although consistency is at the heart of all the client-care initiatives mentioned so far, it never hurts to add in a few surprises. You could host a "thank you" event and invite your top clients. You could send a handpicked gift with a personal note to a client on the anniversary of your first working together. Saying "thank you" and memorializing special relationships is an important element of delivering the ultimate client experience. Consider how you could offer "something special" to each of your top relationships during the year.

Stage six of delivering the ultimate client experience is being spontaneous – occasionally offering something special to your clients, something that really shows them how much you think about them, even when you're not going through the normal course of business. For example, send a book you just finished to your client – just because you think they'd enjoy it, too. Or, maybe host a special event for just some of your top clients where you treat them all like royalty. This is active reciprocity, remembering to say "thank you" and saying it often.

The best way to be spontaneous, though, is to write your thoughts down. When you come up with an idea during the course of your business day, but can't put the idea into action right away, write it down. That way, you won't forget to do that something special. Sure – the things I've mentioned so far might sound elaborate – the book, the special events – but, your gesture doesn't have to be elaborate; it could be as simple as a personalized note you've written and signed yourself that thanks the client for his or her business. Or, it might say, "Hey! I saw you in the paper the other day – you're celebrating your company's anniversary. Congratulations!"

The key is to do it spontaneously, to do it when you think about it, but plan it out in a way that it builds into your communication calendar and really puts that personal attention side to client service we talked about earlier. To give you some ideas to help you be spontaneous, we've provided a lot of guidance in this book and separately, online, in the Encore Library (www.EncorePartners.com/UCEbook). The first is "The Art of a Handwritten Note." It gives you a way to think about making sure you're delivering those personal, spontaneous communications to your best clients on a regular basis. There's also the article, "Client

Gift Idea: Have You Read a Good Book Lately?" These are some great brainstorming ideas that will get you thinking about the ways you can be spontaneous and offer something special to your clients, as you're working to deliver the ultimate client experience.

"Delivering the Ultimate Client Experience" should not be viewed as a laborious chore; it's an opportunity that will lead to your future success. Challenge yourself to implement the six activities outlined above and your business will thrive. Remember – your clients are your greatest assets! Treat them well and the results will be more than you could possibly expect.

Work through these six stages, one at a time, in the priority order you believe will make the biggest difference to your practice. The only caveat: I would define my client segments before I do anything else. That's really the cornerstone for each of the other stages. It's also why, to open this first chapter, I included my own view about finding and attracting the ultimate client. I can promise you, if you make delivering the ultimate client experience a priority for your practice this year, this will be your best year ever. Give me a call, or send me an email if I can help you at all. Most important, take care of your clients by delivering the ultimate client experience and they will take care of you.

Chapter 2:

Make Your Client Profiles Count

Your clients are your most important business asset. To ensure long-term relationships filled with growing opportunities, you need a system for conducting regular client profiles. Profiling helps you offer greater service, uncover new assets, and gain the best referrals. This Chapter introduces you to proven strategies for making meaningful client profiles a part of your practice management routines.

Reading

A simple client profile – asking the right questions in a "different" way – can help you find new opportunities that deepen relationships. Ultimately, you gain a better understanding of your client's total financial picture and personal goals which, in turn, leads to more business!

This chapter will introduce you to another step toward providing the "Ultimate Client Experience." It's a proven process for improving your client profiling, which will lead to:

- Increased assets under management
- An increase in cross-selling opportunities
- A steady stream of referrals

- Greater client loyalty
- More business, the way you enjoy doing business

This book has three goals. First, as with all of our training and coaching sessions at Encore Partners, we want to give you actionable ideas you can put to work right away. We also want to help you focus on delivering the ultimate client experience. There's no better way to grow your business than to take care of your clients. When you service your clients properly, they stay loyal, they achieve their goals, and you do more business and gain more referrals. Client profiling, in particular, helps you deepen and maximize your client relationships. You uncover additional assets and cross-selling opportunities. You gain referrals through advocacy, you build loyalty, and you do more business, the way you enjoy doing your business.

To truly make your client profiles count, to conduct a truly effective profiling campaign, you need to ask and answer five questions:

1. Why profile – or re-profile – your clients?
2. Who will you profile?
3. How will you conduct the profile?
4. What tools do you need to conduct an effective profile?
5. What will you do with your profiling information?

When you ask and answer these questions, your profiling process will move you toward more assets, more sales, more loyalty, and more referrals. As an example – I'm currently doing some coaching work with a financial advisor down in Florida. In getting his action plan together, we decided conducting an effective profiling of *all* his clients was extremely important. He felt he'd lost touch; his clients weren't segmented and his top clients really didn't know everything he could do for them. I'm happy to report that, after just two months of working together, he's on track for a record quarter and his business is up 50% over the same time last year. This is all because he spent more time conducting effective client profiles. I know you'll obtain similar results if you take advantage of the ideas we're discussing here.

Why Profile/Re-Profile Your Clients?

As you consider the prospects of profiling – or re-profiling – clients, you may be wondering why. You might think, "Oh, I know my clients. I know what assets they have, I know what their goals are, and I know the ones who will give me referrals. There's no reason to continuously profile them."

Well, I disagree! I think, to truly deliver the ultimate client experience, you not only need to know what your clients *have*, you also need to be constantly vigilant about what they *want* and, in turn, talk to them about what they *need* – because those things aren't always the same. Profiling, or re-profiling, makes sure you stay up-to-date with your clients. It's the best way to determine the right type of communication to deliver, the right number of communications to send, the right way to really take care of them.

On top of this, when you do a good job of profiling your clients, you clearly define your main client segments. You know who your top clients are; you know who your next-to-top clients are. You know from where your next "A" clients are going to come, among the groups of clients that may not yet be top clients. This helps you deliver different levels of service and communication.

Profiling helps you stay truly current with your top clients. Things change all the time and, just because we talk to our clients on a very regular basis, doesn't mean they always tell us what we need to know. They may have events occurring in their lives that they may not relate to you, as a financial advisor; yet, it really affects the way you help them plan. So – profiling needs to be constant and vigilant. Profiling allows you to evaluate specific new opportunities you may want to make available to your clients – whether it's cross-selling your products or services or doing a satisfaction survey, to determine how you can change or improve the way you're servicing your clients, or to determine how a member of your team is doing. Profiling your clients is at the heart of delivering the ultimate client experience. It can help you set the direction for all the other activities you need to be engaged in, to make that experience meaningful.

Who Will You Profile?

When you get to the point where you're ready to launch a profiling campaign or activity, you need to decide who you'll profile. In this step, you have three choices:

- You can profile all your clients.
- You can profile only your top clients.
- You can profile only a narrow segment of your clients.

Let's start by looking at why you might profile all your clients. Ask yourself several questions:

- Have you segmented your clients?
- When's the last time you did a really good job of segmenting your clients?

- Have you defined your ultimate client relationship? Perhaps you only want to work with one segment of clients. You don't want to have hundreds of clients in multiple segments; you'd rather work with one hundred ultimate relationships. Profiling all your clients can allow you to get to that point.

- Finally, what are your service standards for your multiple client segments? If you haven't profiled your clients, if you haven't defined those segments, it's hard to tell your clients, no matter which segment they're in, what you're going to do for them – or to offer the type of service they want and deserve as members of your clientele.

If you haven't profiled and segmented your clients for a long time – or if you've never profiled and segmented your clients – you need to think about profiling all your clients.

If your clients are already well-segmented, if you already know who your ideal or ultimate clients are, then perhaps, when you think about conducting a profiling exercise or campaign, you want to focus only on your top clients – those folks who generate 70% to 90% of your revenues. As I said earlier, doing this profiling is at the heart of delivering the ultimate client experience. You can't offer your clients service, communication, and care if you don't know what they have, what they want, and what they need.

When you conduct a profiling exercise with your top or ultimate clients, it also gives you a chance to *acknowledge to them their importance to your business.* People like to know how important they are to your practice. You need to let them know this frequently – and you can do this through the profiling process. When you're profiling just your top clients, perhaps your main goal is to spend more time with fewer clients; you want to be the type of advisor who really only has 100 or fewer key relationships. You're going to focus on just those relationships and not try to grow your business to 200 or 300 relationships. As you're profiling them, as you're acknowledging their importance to you, you can update their goals and you can truly understand their priorities. You can uncover new asset opportunities, and you can talk about the advocacy process, which will help you develop high-quality referrals. If you don't need to segment or profile all your clients, then perhaps you should be thinking about how you're going to profile your top clients and what you want to get out of that activity.

A final way to consider running a segmenting activity is to think about focusing on just one of your client segments. Perhaps you have a group of "B" clients or "C" clients who could be "A" clients for your practice. One of the best ways to find out is to go through a profiling activity. Communicate with them, through the profiling process, what an ideal client is and what an ideal client gets from you. You could also use the opportunity, while focusing on a narrow client segment, to do a client survey. What do your clients think about the work you're doing for them? Do they think you're doing as well as you and your team thinks you're doing?

Perhaps you can have a quarterly rotation among your different client segments – in one quarter, you profile your "A" clients, in the second, you profile your "B" clients, and, in the third, you profile your "C" clients. Last, but not least, if you want to find a specific opportunity to cross-sell, capture assets, or build referrals, you may be profiling only one segment of your clientele.

The most important thing you can do when considering who you'll profile is to make sure you decide on a way to approach profiling in your business; you can't leave it to chance. The greatest mistakes in client management are not having a system for segmenting clients, not committing to service levels, and forgetting to communicate regularly. Profiling kicks that process off.

How Will You Conduct the Profiling?

Let's move to our third question: how you compose the profiles. You really have three choices:

- In person
- Through mail or email
- A combination of the two

Most often, you conduct in-person profiling when meeting with your top clients as part of your annual or quarterly review. You may also conduct in-person profiling with potential "A" clients – people you think may understand what it takes to become an ultimate client of your practice. We recommend that, when composing in-person profiles, you send out a letter, along with a copy of your profiling questionnaire, in advance of that meeting. The letter talks about the fact that the profile is important and why you're doing it. It also asks the person you'll be meeting with to complete as much of the questionnaire as they can so, when you get together, you can finish it off. That way, they're fully prepared for that meeting. We give you a copy of an ultimate client profiling letter in Appendix 1, "Client Letters and Client Profile Form."

Sometimes, profiling is equally successful when it's done just through mail or email. This is usually the case when you're targeting some information you want to draw from your clientele – targeted profiling for cross-selling opportunities, for introducing new services, for capturing more assets, for doing a client survey, getting feedback on how your clients think you're doing. The key to these mail-only or email-only profiles is they are very brief and very easy to answer – perhaps with less than 10 questions, which are mostly multiple choice or "rate what you think about this potential product" or "how am I doing?" questions.

Finally, you may have decided already that you want to profile all your clients. You want to segment your book of business. If this is the case, using a combination of mail and in-person meetings is most appropriate. Here, as opposed to meeting with all your top clients after sending them profile questionnaires in advance, so they get used to it, you're asking your client to fill in and return that profile to you. You're not going to take any action with them until they send their profile back. Fully 40 to 60% of your clients will send you that profile, giving you an opportunity to look it over and call them to hold an in-person meeting. We give you the tools to enable you to conduct this type of profile in Appendix 1, "Client Letters and Client Profile Form."

What Tools Do You Need to Compose an Effective Profile?

In reviewing how you might conduct a profiling campaign, we referenced question four: what tools do you need to conduct an effective profile? You need three tools:

- An introductory letter
- Good listening skills
- A thorough questionnaire

Your introductory letter would be included when you're sending the questionnaire out to your top clients, because you're doing an ultimate client profile only. An introductory letter is needed when you're segmenting/profiling all your clients. An introductory letter is needed if you're surveying your clients. Samples of all three letters are included in Appendix 1, "Client Letters and Client Profile Form."

You also need great listening skills. Remember – we want you to be talking with your clients, not only about what they think they want, but also about what they need. Sometimes, those two things are completely different. By listening well, by pointing out to your clients what they're saying, you can help them clear that up. It makes your job easier and it makes it easier for them to accomplish their long-term goals.

Finally, you need to have a great questionnaire. Of course, you want to ask traditional questions – but you need to ask them in a different way, in a way that really gets your clients talking about what they want, what they need, and what their dreams are.

You would use a full questionnaire, if you were conducting a complete profile; you can have specialized questionnaires when you're looking for new sales or service opportunities. And, of course, you can have client surveys.

Next, let's look at how you might go through a questionnaire – both from a listening perspective and from the perspective of the questionnaire itself. How can you ask those traditional questions in different ways?

1. The easiest way to begin a profiling process – whether you're doing it through the mail or in person – is to ask simple

questions. We always suggest you start out by making sure you have updated personal information on your clients. This is easy information for them to give. It gets the conversation started, but it can also be very critical to the way you communicate with your clients. What form of communication do your clients like to receive most often – through mail or email, in-person, or do they prefer to be called on their cell phone? You can gather this information by asking a simple question to get the conversation started.

2. Another simple question to use at the beginning of a profiling interview or profiling questionnaire is, "Have there been any changes to your employment-related information?" It's good to know your client's current position in their company or firm. It may help you in your networking and prospecting opportunities. From a financial planning and compliance perspective, updating your customers' annual income is extremely important. Also – what about their retirement planning? How much money do they have in their company-sponsored retirement plans? Can you help them with it now, through an in-service withdrawal? Are they planning retirement over the near term? When is the last time you asked your client when they want to retire? Have they brought that date any closer or have they extended it any further? This is very important information to have as you're keeping up with all your clients but, in particular, with your top clients.

3. If you're doing a thorough questionnaire, you may also want to build in some survey questions. We like to do this in the front of the questionnaire, in order to keep the process going smoothly. Ask how your clients think you're doing. Have them

rate you on service, communication, and your understanding of their goals. Ask where they think you can improve your service and what your strengths are. This will allow you to head off problems, to keep small problems from becoming big ones. It will also help you improve and communicate your service standards, if the clients don't understand the level of service you can offer to them. Through this process, you may discover that a member of your team is excelling at their work – and that's an opportunity to reward a teammate for taking good care of a client. This can also be the basis for a client survey. Please refer to the sample profiling form (questionnaire), in Appendix 1, "Client Letters and Client Profile Form."

4. Of course, no questionnaire or profile would be complete if you didn't talk about financial and investment goals and objectives. Here again, however, you want to ask your questions in creative ways. You want to be sure you really understand what your clients' investment objectives are; in fact, you want to be sure that your *clients* truly understand what their investment objectives are! Sometimes, they say one thing, but act completely differently: they say they want income, but they don't need it; they say they want growth, but they invest in income-oriented investments. This gives you an opportunity to discuss key holdings. It also gives you a basis to update your asset allocations or your estate-planning analysis.

5. As long as you're talking about goals and objectives, you also need to talk about risk concerns. An interesting way to talk about risk concerns is to relate them to interest rates or to movements in stock markets. Ask your clients how they think

their investments or loans will change if the market goes one way or another, or if interest rates go one way or another. This truly helps you understand how sophisticated your clients are in thinking about their personal risk profiles. It helps you finalize or firm up time horizons for achieving specific investments and goals. It helps you understand whether your clients think about return from an absolute perspective or from a relative perspective. It continues to help you talk with them about asset allocation and estate planning. Again, ask questions that are basic to any new account form or profiling exercise, but in a different way – so you have logical, open and honest communication.

6. How have your clients' thoughts changed, as related to their longer-term planning, since the last time you went through a similar profiling exercise? Have they updated their wills, trusts, or their life insurance policies, and not told you about it? How does that affect the way you work with them? What could or should you be doing, to help them execute those plans? Do they have any new financial goals? Perhaps something has happened in their lives and they're thinking differently about how they want to plan for their future. They're thinking differently about retirement, education planning, or about their charitable giving.

There's a lot of confusion around what people can do with IRAs, rollovers, required minimum distributions or contribution levels – have you talked with your clients about that? What about their income tax concerns – has their tax status changed in the last year, or since the last time you profiled them? What are the long-term-planning issues going through your clients' minds during the course of the year – plans they may not have discussed with you? When you spend time talking about longer-term planning, it helps you really uncover new opportunities in the best way – in a way that not only helps you earn more money, but also helps your clients execute on their goals and plans in a way that will help them be more successful.

7. We believe one of the best ways to build referrals is through client advocacy. It's letting your clients know that you grow your practice through careful selection of new clients or through referrals from current clients. You specifically list, during your profiling process, the people that you believe your client knows they could give you a referral to. It takes a little bit of up-front homework, but cuts down on the randomness of asking for referrals. It gives you the right type of referrals you need to grow your business. It's a very important strategy and a client profiling meeting can be a great place to implement it.

8. The best way to end a client profiling meeting is to come to mutual agreement on key findings. During the dialog you've had, as you've gone through the questionnaire, as you've gone through the profile, you've identified certain things you and your client need to readdress, as one or both of you gather more information. List those at the end of your profile – one to five key findings you want to make a priority for your follow-up. What additional information is required to accomplish these key findings? Perhaps your clients need to give you more statements, a tax return, some information about their company retirement plan? List those things and get a commitment to the key findings and the additional

information that's required. It'll make the meeting seem more important and the follow-up much easier.

What Will You Do With Your Profiling Information?

The last question you need to answer, to make your client profiles count, is: what will you do with your profiling information? Of course, this may seem obvious. If a sales opportunity arises; you'll take care of it. If a service improvement idea arises, you'll take care of it. Unfortunately, after a client profile is completed, we sometimes forget to follow up, because we get so busy with other stuff that keeps us busy every day. Make that follow-up a priority! If you don't, you're wasting the time you invested conducting that profiling; not only are you wasting your own time, you're also wasting your client's time.

Let's look at the process of conducting that top client, in-person profiling exercise. You send out the letter – along with a copy of the questionnaire – and you've told your clients you're going to call them, to schedule a meeting. Remember, these are your top clients – potentially your ultimate clients. *Make sure you call them within five days* of mailing that letter, to schedule that appointment. Even if they have to put it off for a while, keep your commitments. In the meeting itself, go through an agenda. Conduct an organized meeting. Once the profiling meeting is over, send them a thank-you note. In that thank-you note, outline the key findings – those next steps you agreed to during the profiling process. If you're really working with your high-end clients – your most important clients – you might even include a small gift, along with that thank-you note, memorializing the importance of conducting these regular profiling meetings, to help you really help your clients work through the process of achieving their long-term personal financial goals.

Finally, be sure you reconnect with each person you've met with who has key findings within two weeks of the meeting. Make that asset allocation adjustment recommendation. Offer that new service you discussed during the interview. Refer them to other necessary professionals, to help them to accomplish some goals that were uncovered. Give them feedback as to how you overcame the service obstacle they saw in your practice. Tell them how the referral process is going with the people they referred to you. Again – make sure this process is fluid.

To really be sure your client profiling is effective with your top clients, the follow-up is as important as spending the individual time going through the profile with the client. And – of course – repeat this process at least annually.

If your profiling campaign is a client segmentation campaign, then you're not calling anybody for an appointment until they send that profiling questionnaire back to you. But, when they send it back, call immediately to schedule that appointment, to keep your commitment to your client. Once you have that appointment, the rest of the follow-up is the same as described earlier, talking about top clients doing that in-person profiling exercise. Make sure you do that follow-up just the same way. Remember – only 40 to 60% of people you send questionnaires to will send them back. If people don't send the questionnaire back to you, resend them after 60 days and another 40 to 60% will respond. This allows you to cover your client base very effectively with just a couple of mailings over a two-month period of time. If you're not comfortable with how you're doing with your segmenting – if the first round doesn't work out quite as well as you would have liked – repeat this process annually.

When you're conducting client surveys or targeted profile exercises, be sure you respond to the answers you get. Read between the lines: look for service opportunities and uncover sales opportunities. Remember that, sometimes, what you observe in a survey or a profile is really a sign of something more your client wants to tell you. Take advantage of that opportunity.

And – by all means – *always* send a thank-you letter. One of the best ways to get continued responses to your surveys and profiling activities is to constantly say, "Thank you." This lets your clients know the process you're going through – even if it's a simple survey – is important to the way you run your business.

Those were the five steps – the five questions you need to work through when you're considering conducting a client profiling campaign. Client profiling is vitally important. It will give you an opportunity to uncover new ways in which you can deliver greater service to your clients and, in turn, win more business. Sometimes, it's more appropriate to conduct profiling campaigns with all your clients; sometimes it's more appropriate to be more focused – but, however you decide to do it, make sure you use the right type of tools, ask the right questions, and ask them in the right way, to get the right information and make it truly effective, then conduct a follow-up and say, "Thank you." If you really want the profiling process to work for you, it needs to be a continuous process that you work through consistently.

Ultimate Clients Letters

Overview

1. The goals of this campaign are to be sure your best clients *know* they're your best clients, to uncover additional business opportunities and to begin building the basis for regular referrals or references to members of their affinity groups and attract more ultimate clients.

2. Create a list of your best clients, as discussed in this chapter.

3. At the rate of five to ten per week, mail the Ultimate Client Letter and the Preferred Client Profile until all your top clients receive them. Include your brochure or resume and a return envelope.

4. Call each client within five business days from the day you mailed them the letter and profile, to schedule a time to review the profile in person.

5. In reviewing the questionnaire with the client, be sure to focus on identifying new financial goals, new assets you may be able to manage, and how you may be able to encourage referrals to members of their affinity groups.

6. Follow this meeting up with a personalized thank-you note or gift.

7. If you have uncovered specific investment or service needs, be sure to follow up.

8. Call the client after two weeks and mention specific names of people to whom you would like to be referred, or to be able to use the client's name as a referrer when contacting them.

Ultimate Clients Profile Cover Letter

<Mr./Ms>. *<ultimate client name>*

<address>

Dear *<ultimate client first name>*,

A Special Thank You and Update

As we begin a new *<year/quarter>*, *<I/we>* wanted to take time to thank you for being such an important part of *<my/our>* practice. In addition to being appreciative of the business we've done together, your loyalty and willingness to share your time and ideas have added greatly to the way *<I/we>* do business with all of *<my/our>* clients. You've helped put perspective on the investment environment in a way that helps remind *<me/us>* of how important the work *<I/we>* do is to the financial well-being of *<my/our>* clients.

Though we talk fairly often, *<I/we>* also want to sit down with you and be certain *<I/we>* have a thorough understanding of all your goals and objectives. To that end, please find enclosed a Preferred Client Profile that you can either send back before we meet, or that we can review at our meeting. The information obtained from this questionnaire will help *<me/us>* continue doing the kind of work for you that you've come to expect.

<assistant's name> will call you early next week to set a time. Thank you again for your advocacy.

Sincerely-

<your name>

P.S. Please don't let the profile overwhelm you. Though it may seem lengthy, it's one way <*I/we*> can be certain you, as an important client, receive the type of service you deserve. We can always finish it when we meet.

Mail-in Profile Cover Letter

<Mr./Ms.> <*client name*>
<*address*>

Dear <*client first name*>,

Thank You and Update

As we begin the new <*year/quarter*>, <*I/we*> wanted to take time to thank you for being an important part of <*my/our*> investment practice. As you know, <*I/we*> believe in understanding your total financial picture, to ensure <*I am/we are*> presenting the best solutions to help you achieve your goals.

To that end, <*I/we*> would like to sit down with you and be certain <*I/we*> have a thorough understanding of all of your goals and objectives. Please complete the attached profile and return it to <*me/us*> in the enclosed return envelope. Once <*I/we*> receive your information, <*I/we*> will call you to set up a meeting. We can then more thoroughly review your goals, answer questions and set direction for the next twelve months.

Financial needs can change frequently as we move through life. The information obtained from this profile and our meeting will help maximize <*my/our*> understanding of your financial aspirations, and help <*me/us*> present the best possible solutions as we work together in the years to come.

Thank you again for your advocacy.

Sincerely,

<your name>

P.S. Please don't let the profile overwhelm you. Though it may seem lengthy, it's one way *<I/we>* can be certain you, as an important client, receive the type of service you deserve. We can always finish it when we meet.

Client Profile Questionnaire

Please see Appendix 1, "Client Letters and Client Profile Form," for more client letters and for the Client Profile questionnaire.

Chapter 3:

Is It Time to Clean Up Your Orphan Assets?

Asset-gathering can sometimes be a double-edged sword. As overall assets grow, there's a tendency to take on new assets over which you may have little knowledge or control. Over time, these orphan assets may lead to difficulties in properly monitoring your clients' holdings, measuring investment performance, controlling taxes, and performing a myriad of other client-focused activities. Cleaning out your orphan assets may sound tedious, but we know from experience it will put you in a position to increase client contact and to advance your operating efficiencies. This Chapter gives you a 5-step process for running an orphan asset campaign designed to boost production and improve client service.

Reading

> *"True generosity is a duty as indispensably necessary as those imposed on us by law."*
>
> *—Oliver Goldsmith*

One of your main focuses as a financial advisor is asset-gathering. Whether your specialty is financial planning, estate protection, or investment management, you generally strive to aggregate your clients' investments, savings, and insurance polices. This basic strategy allows you to both provide a high level of service to your clients and to build an asset base that generates growing revenues for you and for your team.

Over time, however, most financial advisors tend to accumulate a few orphan assets – stray holdings that are more trouble than they're worth. Though you may have accepted the responsibility for oversight of these stray holdings with the best of intentions, such orphan assets will eventually drag on your time and ability to care for your clients.

The ongoing discipline of your client-management process should help you minimize orphan assets but, over time, client indecision or your lack of persistence may allow them to get ahead of you. If you find yourself with too many positions on your books, we recommend running a campaign to pro-actively reposition these assets. This is not to suggest making changes for the sake of change – and a quick new commission or fee. As a financial professional, you have a group of products or services over which you've completed thorough due diligence and which you feel most comfortable recommending to your clients. Converting your orphan assets into these preferred positions is important for your client relationships. You'll have more time for your clients, increase the overall quality of their holdings, and be in a position to monitor their assets more effectively. At the same time, this campaign can be a springboard to increased production, monetarily rewarding you for the time you invest in this activity.

What follows is a 5-step process for running an orphan asset campaign. As you look for activities to increase your production and add more value to your client relationships, put this idea to work. The results will be significant.

1. **Build a list of your orphan assets**

   For those of you who hold the majority of your clients' assets on the books of your broker/dealer or custodian, we recommend compiling a report listing all your holdings, from smallest to largest. The majority of the positions you'll be reviewing will show up on the first pages of this report. If your clients' investments and policies are held at mutual fund and insurance companies, you may be able to run a similar report by accessing your client data through these companies' Websites. Others may have aggregation software for managing client relationships; use this tool to build a report of outlying holdings. Finally, if these automated options aren't at your disposal, devise a plan for manually capturing this information. Perhaps you could ask a member of your staff to go through the binders and files in which you compile your clients' holdings. No matter which option you choose, build your list before moving on to the next steps.

2. **Decide on a campaign style**

   Your orphan asset campaign could be a short-term project, conducted over a concentrated time period – or you might choose to work through this process gradually, as you conduct regular client reviews and meetings. Either way, you need to decide on a methodology for conducting pro-active discussions with your clients. These suggestions can be implemented by you, by members of your team, or by a combination of the two.

- "Call me" campaign – This campaign style requires printing individual statements that list orphan holdings, circling or highlighting the positions in question and then mailing the statements to your clients with a note to call you to review the items you've marked. When your clients call you for discussion, you can either take the call or have your assistant schedule a time for a telephone appointment. You should work this out with your assistant in advance. This process displays your concern for your clients' well being – you're letting them know you've been reviewing their statements and that you've isolated an issue important enough to warrant a note and call. One caveat: don't send too many notes at one time – you may be overwhelmed with calls. Start with 5 to 10 notes per day.

- Sales or marketing assistant calls – If you have a registered sales or marketing assistant, you could delegate the task of calling your clients who have orphan positions. These calls are the quickest way to move through the process of addressing orphan accounts. Be sure to give your assistant a script with specific instructions, for letting your clients know he/she is making recommendations on your behalf. Your assistant should also use this call to determine if there are service needs, as well as to arrange a call time or appointment for you, if they uncover new opportunities. This technique has 3 benefits: you leverage your time, your clients receive another service touch, and your assistant becomes more familiar with your clientele.

- "By the way" campaign – If you're reluctant to dedicate blocks of specific time for this activity, consider a "by the way" campaign. Here, you simply keep a list of your orphan assets on your desk. When you're speaking with a client on the phone or in-person, you refer to this list, to determine if they have holdings that need review. If so, you simply say, "by the way, I was reviewing your holdings and noticed you own…" Again, it helps your clients understand your attention to detail and may lead to new business or service opportunities.

3. Develop a timeline

Projects almost always achieve better results when they're planned in advance, with specific timelines. Even if you choose to implement a more 'laissez faire' approach, you should set a deadline for working though all your orphan positions. One of the best ways to determine time frames is to total up the number of calls that need to be made or letters that need to be written and divide them by the number of business days over which you want to accomplish this task. For example, if you have 100 calls to make and want to be finished in a month, plan on making 5 calls per day.

4. Assign responsibilities

As with any campaign, you need to communicate your plan of action to everyone on your team. Even if certain team members aren't specifically involved in this process, they should understand your goals, so they can support the efforts of those who are required to build the list, send the letters, or make and take phone calls. Besides – often times, discussing an idea like this one will lead to additional ideas for improving sales and service.

5. **Measure your results**

In the end, you need to determine if this effort has paid dividends to your practice. If it does, perhaps you'll decide to run this campaign twice per year. If not, drop it or tweak it; a campaign that doesn't work shouldn't be used again. Important metrics to include in your evaluation could be: letters sent, number of contacts, new sales, service enhancement opportunities, appointments scheduled, and number of orphan positions that were re-positioned.

Cleaning out your orphan assets may sound tedious and unproductive, but we know from experience that any activity that puts you in a position to increase client contact and to advance your operating efficiencies will have a long-term payoff. From a boost in production, to improving the way you monitor your clients' holdings, pro-actively re-positioning orphan assets is a winning idea.

Chapter 4:

Simple Report Card Client Surveys: Are You Making the Grade?

Allowing your clients to grade your performance is an essential step in delivering the ultimate client experience. A focused client survey can show you where you shine, as well as point out areas in need of improvement. This chapter gives you a simple formula for conducting a client survey.

Reading

Client surveys are "report cards" for assessing your effectiveness. They're an essential component of delivering the ultimate client experience. If you haven't surveyed your clients in a while, there's no better time than the present.

1. **Decide whose feedback you'd like to solicit at this time, and put your list together:**

   Generally speaking, the more feedback you receive the better off you and your team will be. At the same time, every report card that comes back with a suggestion or question will need follow-up.

Given all of your other time commitments, you'll need to decide if you should survey your entire client base or just a select group of top clients. If you go with a select group, consider scheduling the remainder of your clientele in future months.

2. **Determine the structure of your report card, create a rough draft and secure any required approvals:**

Here your choice is to only solicit report card-style feedback, or to include your report card in a client profile update. If you've recently completed thorough client profiles, stick with a simple report card. If you're getting ready to sit down with your clients to conduct regular reviews, make the report card a part of your process.

3. **Begin putting the report cards in the hands of your clients:**

In this step, your options are a written correspondence (mail or email), an in-person meeting, or a combination of both. The simple report card is best done by mail, whereas a client profile may be done all 3 ways.

4. **Follow-up on all questions and concerns:**

This should go without saying but, all too often, we find advisors get so busy with their daily routines they forget to properly respond to this important client feedback. We suggest setting aside time each day to review your report cards or profiles with your assistant (or team), to determine priority and assign follow-up responsibilities with a deadline.

5. **Send a thank you to all responders:**

This simple gesture will help further impress upon your clients the importance of their feedback. These replies should be personally written "thank you" notes. Whenever possible, make mention of follow-up you'll be doing, to answer questions or to alleviate concerns identified on the report card. If you choose to use a form letter, at least make sure it's personalized and signed by hand.

Depending on the approach you select, these five steps can easily be accomplished over a 30- to 60-day time period. You'll end up with valuable information for improving your practice, as well as new business and referral opportunities. *When was the last time your received a report card? Maybe it's time to ask for one!*

Sample Client Report Card and Letter

Dear <*personalize*>,

Do you remember receiving report cards? These "progress reviews," no matter how much you studied or didn't study, brought on a certain amount of apprehension. Top students sometimes fretted they wouldn't maintain their high marks while those who were averse to schoolwork hoped they would avoid disaster. The outcome usually wasn't worth the worry and simply resulted in setting a fresh direction for future efforts.

As you're such a valued client of our practice, we'd like to solicit your feedback, by asking you to complete the attached "Client Report Card." This brief survey will only take a few minutes of your time. It will help us build on those aspects of our business that are working well and improve on any areas where you may see a need for improvement. There's no better way for us to provide the type of service and advice you deserve than to be sure we understand your expectations.

Should you have any questions, or if you wish to discuss your ideas personally, please feel free to give us a call. Otherwise, we've enclosed a postage paid envelope for your convenience.

Thanks in advance for your input!

Sincerely,

<sign by hand>

<your name>

P.S. We have a few openings for new client additions to our practice. If you know anyone who might benefit from our work, please let us know, or give them our name.

Client Report Card

On a scale of 1 to 5, with 1 meaning "needs improvement," and 5 meaning "we are meeting your expectations," how would you rate us on the following categories?

1. Service – our responsiveness to your inquiries

_____ Overall team service

_____ My personal service

_____ (list other team members) service

Are you aware of any outstanding service issues?

1.

2.

2. Communication, frequency of contact

_____ Contact by telephone

_____ Communication by mail/email

_____ In-person meetings

Would you like to be on our private email list? (circle one): **Yes No**

If so, please list your email address here

_____.

Should we be in contact more, less, or about the same amount throughout the year?

Communication suggestions:

3. Advice, properly understand your goals

_____ Investment and financial goals

_____ Tolerance for risk

_____ Personal goals and objectives

Have there been any changes in your personal or financial circumstances of which we should be aware? (circle one) Yes No

If yes, please explain:

Please use the space below to indicate any additional areas where you see *need for improvement*.

Please use the space below to list what you believe to be our *strengths*.

We believe it's important to recognize members of our team who are *exceeding your expectations*. Please list any names below, along with your comments.

Would you like us to *call you*, to discuss this report card or any other questions relating to our work together? (circle one): Yes   No

References – We have a few openings for new client additions to our practice. If you know anyone who might benefit from our work, please let us know, or give them our name.

Chapter 5:

Delivering the Ultimate Client Experience: New Year Letter and Profiling Exercise

> The more time you spend with your clients, the better service you'll provide and the more income you'll derive. As the next financial year gets underway, you may be planning your client communication calendar for the entire year. At the very least, you should decide how you'll touch your top clients at least 24 times throughout the year – letters, emails, calls, and special events. Studies have shown that high net-worth clients expect – and deserve – this level of attention. A New Year Letter can set the tone for the entire year.

Reading

January is generally a month in which financial advisors send their clients a New Year communication; it's also an excellent time to conduct reviews and re-profile relationships. This letter gives you a chance to say "thank you," reflect on the past year, and offer a glimpse into the coming year. Profiling helps you segment your clientele, uncover new business opportunities and promote referrals.

This chapter gives you complete instructions for a New Year profiling campaign, as well as a sample letter – see Appendix 1, "Client Letters and Client Profile Form." You could use the letter in its current format, or you could alter it, to include other important ideas you'd like to share with your clients. To help with profiling, we also include two versions of our "Next Financial Year Wealth Management Profile." These questionnaires provide you with tools for gathering updated information from your clients. Send the profile along with the letter or use it when you're conducting an individual review.

One of our goals at Encore Partners is to show our clients how to deliver the ultimate client experience. In this chapter, we'll focus on helping you make the most of your client relationships. Use these tools and exercises to add value, to build loyalty, and to grow your personal income.

New Year Profiling Experience

Option 1: Utilize the second letter as a template for a New Year letter to your clients and set the stage for beginning-of-the-year client review meetings. Be sure to customize the letter, to fit your business style and personality. Personal salutations and signatures will elevate its importance and improve your clients' receptiveness.

Option 2: Combine your New Year letter with a profiling exercise. The goals of this optional campaign are to set the stage for beginning-of-the-year client review meetings, to better segment your clients, to uncover additional business opportunities, and to build the basis for regular referrals or references.

Action Steps for Option 2:

1. Determine which of your clients will be included:

- If you've already segmented your clientele, you may only want to run this campaign with your top segments.
- If you need to segment or improve your segmentation, run this campaign with all your clients.

2. Personalize and mail one of the client letters in the appendix to your selected client group:

- Client Letter One One is intended to be very straightforward and offers no commentary.
- Client Letter Two is written to be friendlier and provides the client with more background.
- Select and customize one of these two letters, based on your practice style and other communications you may have already sent or planned.
- Both letters provide an option for including your "The Next Financial Year Wealth Profile Update" questionnaire. This option will give you a head start for gathering updated information for your client review meetings.
- The second letter contains optional verbiage, if you'd rather not include the profile with the letter and simply wait to complete it during your review meetings.

3. Call clients who return the profile within 5 days of receipt, to set an appointment to review their responses:

- In reviewing the profile with the client, your objective is to determine mutually agreed-upon "key findings." These findings are your action steps for managing each relationship.

- Focus on identifying and gathering new assets, new financial goals, and cross-selling opportunities. Look for how you may be able to encourage advocacy and referrals.

- Follow each meeting up with a personalized "thank you" letter that includes "key findings." There is an example in Appendix 1.

- If you uncover specific investment or service needs, be sure to bring them to closure within two weeks. Schedule follow-up meetings when necessary.

- Use the information you've gathered, to segment clients for ongoing communication and service.

4. **Non-Responders – send a reminder letter with the profile form after 30 days and again after 60 days, if required.**

5. **Repeat this process at least annually.**

Chapter 6:

Delivering the Ultimate Client Experience: Tax Planning Letter and Tip Sheet

Helping your clients organize their tax information presents you with a chance to provide a value-added service, while potentially uncovering new business opportunities. This chapter gives you a tax planning "tip sheet" template for a personal client letter.

Reading

By the end of winter, your clients have received the majority of their important tax filing documentation. One way to add value to your important relationships is to offer assistance in organizing this information. This activity can also put you in a position to uncover additional assets and to present cross-selling ideas.

Neither document offers tax advice – only organizational suggestions, along with financial and investment planning discussion items. The letter can be utilized in its current format, or it could alternatively include language to schedule a formal review meeting.

The "tip sheet" should be included with the letter. It can be mailed without plans for follow-up, or you may choose to use it as a discussion-starter. Topics ranging from IRAs and retirement plans to annuities and municipal bonds are logical extensions of the questions asked in the "tip sheet." Each question is prefaced with a relevant category from basic tax filing forms and schedules.

If one of your goals in the next financial year is to deliver a higher level of client service and contact, this letter and "tip sheet" will add to your efforts.

Tip Sheet Letter

Dear *<personalize>*,

Organizing Your Tax Information

"The hardest thing to understand in the world is the income tax."

—Albert Einstein

This is the time of year when you receive forms and schedules for filing your income taxes. Some of these reports are the result of our relationship, while others are generated by your employer, various financial institutions with which you do business, or private business ventures. Knowing what to expect and which items are required, to file your taxes on a timely basis, can be difficult.

<omit the next sentence if you're a tax preparer> The tax preparation forms you receive from your accountant can be helpful but, with the complexities of an ever-changing tax code, they can be just as

overwhelming as the Form 1040 itself. With this in mind, we're writing to offer you our "Tax Planning Tip Sheet." We hope you'll put it to good use.

Whether you file your own income taxes or use the assistance of a tax professional – our recommended preference – this tip sheet is designed to make your tax season less stressful. We believe properly organizing your forms, schedules, and records can make tax filing simpler. Our tip sheet may also help you avoid unnecessary delays and extensions.

Finally, this is an ideal time of year to review tax-related investment and wealth planning issues. Each category outlined in the tip sheet contains questions you should relate to your current financial plan. Please let us know if there are any items we need to discuss in further detail.

All the best,

<your name>

Tax Planning Tip Sheet

Properly organizing your forms, schedules, and records can make tax filing simpler. It should also help you avoid unnecessary delays and extensions. Whether you file your own taxes or use a tax professional – our recommended preference – this tip sheet is designed to make your tax season less stressful.

Additionally, this is an ideal time of year to review tax-related investment and wealth planning issues. Each category below contains questions you should relate to your current financial plan. Please let us know if there are any items we need to discuss.

Track Your Income Sources

1. **Do you have records for all of your sources of "earned" income?**

   This category includes your employment earnings, as well as business-related income.

   - Did this total materially change – up or down – in the current financial year?
   - Do you expect significant changes in the next financial year?

2. **Have you received summaries and schedules from the financial institutions with which you do business?**

   This category includes banks, credit unions, brokerage firms, mutual funds, and other investments. In addition to forms like 1099s, you should also be sure you have profit and loss statements that list capital gains for your investment accounts.

   - Are you satisfied with the current interest rates on your savings accounts, CDs, and other fixed income investments?
   - Are your investments keeping you on track with your financial goals?

3. **Did you receive any miscellaneous income during the current financial year?**

   This category includes rental, royalty, trust, partnership, social security, and farm income, as well as alimony. Also, consider whether or not you received distributions from IRAs or other retirement plans, such as pensions and 401ks.

   - Would you like a second opinion on the performance of your company retirement and IRA accounts?

- Do you need to consider additional planning for Required Minimum Distributions or other withdrawals from your retirement accounts?

4. **Don't forget to track your tax exempt and tax deferred income and investments.**

This category includes municipal bonds and bond funds, along with insurance programs and annuities.

- Are you unnecessarily paying taxes on income from investments that you don't currently use?
- Have you considered updating these investments, to take of advantage of new income and principle protection options?

Review Potential Deductions

5. **Do you have any business related expenses?**

This grouping primarily includes self-employment-related expenses, but could also include such categories as reservist or educator expenses. Self-employment income may afford you tax-saving opportunities, even if your work is only part-time.

- Do you have any self-employment income – consulting, weekend business, etc.?
- Have you reviewed newer retirement plan options which give individuals with self-employment income more flexibility and increased deductions?

6. **Are you eligible for deductions related to education expenses?**

This category is composed of student loan interest or deductions for tuition and fees.

- Should we review the performance and suitability of your current custodial, 529, or other education savings accounts?

- Do you need to review new educational savings options for yourself, your children, or grandchildren?

7. Did you participate in a Health Savings Account?

This relatively new healthcare option combines high-deductible health insurance with a tax-deductible savings account, similar to an IRA.

- Have you checked to see if this option is available to you through your employer?
- If so, is it right for you?

8. Are you thoroughly reviewing your itemized expenses?

This category includes medical and dental expenses, interest paid, charitable contributions, and job expenses.

- Have you reviewed your debt portfolio, for tax and interest savings opportunities?

9. Did you make contributions to IRAs or retirement plans?

This category includes IRAs, 401k plans, and deferred compensation plans.

- Have you selected the right IRA account?
- Should you consolidate your IRA and rollover accounts?
- Have you taken maximum advantage of your retirement plan savings options?
- Are you satisfied with the asset allocation in your 401k account?
- Does your 401k allow for "in-service" withdrawals?

We hope you found this tip sheet to be helpful. Please let us know if there are any investment management or financial planning issues we need to review further.

Chapter 7:

Delivering the Ultimate Client Experience: Client Care Letter and Mid-year Profile

> The volatility of the stock market, big swings in interest rates and other economic news and trends can put clients on edge. This chapter provides you with a letter that may help reduce this anxiety. Additionally, we give you a brief client update form, to help you uncover needs and plan for the remainder of the coming financial year.

Special Notes

1. This letter and update form are appropriate for all segments of your clientele.
2. You may choose to send this letter by itself or along with the update questionnaire. If you use the questionnaire, be sure to include a return envelope.
3. Be sure to personalize the salutation and sign by hand.
4. You should include a couple of handwritten sentences, in a "P.S." section, when sending this letter to your ultimate clients.

Letter

Dear <personalize>,

"Wall Street people learn nothing and forget everything."

These words are from Benjamin Graham, often called the "Dean of Wall Street" and the father of value investing. They're worth repeating, given the dramatic swings we've been experiencing in the stock market. One day, the "experts" are convinced, by their analysis of a key economic report, that interest rates are headed lower – and the stock market soars. A few days later, these same "experts" reinterpret the very same information but, this time, it leads to a major stock market sell-off.

Although this volatility may make for good news headlines, we find it discomforting, because we know it causes unneeded apprehension among our clients. No matter how confident you may be in your long-term financial and investment planning, it's only natural to be a little nervous when interest rates are rising, gas prices are spiking, housing prices are leveling and the stock market is having an identity crisis. Intellectually, you might believe everything will be okay but, emotionally, you may feel challenged.

Don't forget – this is one of the areas in which we stand ready to assist you. In addition to managing your money and monitoring your financial plan, we're your sounding board for questions, concerns, and commentaries. Sometimes, talking through the news of the day can help you rest easier. Please call if you'd like to schedule a time to speak by phone, or to get together for an impromptu review, before our next regular appointment.

Finally, as we enter the dog days of August, it's an important time of year to update your records and to determine if you've uncovered any special financial planning needs. Attached to this letter, you'll find a brief questionnaire with a few quick tax, gift, and investment planning questions. Take a few minutes to fill it out and return it in the enclosed envelope. If you prefer to personally discuss these questions, give us a call, so we can arrange a mutually convenient time to get together.

The world of investments and financial planning is filled with interruptions and distractions. We believe open communication, along with a steady commitment to understanding changing needs, will help us successfully work together for many years to come. Thank you for the confidence you place in us by allowing us to be a part of your long-term planning team.

All the best,

<sign by hand>

<your name>

Mid-Year Client Update Form

Thank you for taking the time to complete this update.

Feel free to use the back of these pages or extra paper if necessary.

Have there been any changes to your employment related information?

Employer:	
Your current position:	
Your annual income (salary, bonus, other):	

Should we anticipate any special tax considerations in the next financial year?

Examples: bonuses, raises, extraordinary business losses, capital gains.

Please describe:

Are you planning to make any special family or charitable gifts before the end of the next financial year? If yes, please describe:

Are you familiar with the increased gifting limits for the next financial year?

Circle one: Yes No

Do you need our assistance in selecting the most tax-advantaged gifting strategies?

Circle one: Yes No

Do you have a company-sponsored retirement plan(s) on which you'd like a second opinion?

Circle one: Yes No

If yes, please fill in details:

Type (Pension, 401k, deferred compensation, other):	
Indicate self or spouse plan.	
Current Value:	
Is there anything else you feel we should know?	

Have you updated your wills, trusts, life insurance policies or other estate planning tools during the past year? If so, which ones?

Have you begun or are you considering planning for any new financial goals, including but not limited to retirement planning, education planning, estate planning, or charitable giving?

Do you hold any retirement, investment, or savings accounts which we may not be aware of and on which you'd like a second opinion? If yes, please list below:

There have been several tax law changes relating to IRA contribution limits, rollover considerations, and minimum required distributions. Should we spend time reviewing your IRAs, rollover accounts, and company-sponsored retirement plans? Please list any specific concerns or considerations:

How are we doing?

On a scale of 1 to 10, with 1 meaning "needs improvement" and 10 meaning we are exceeding your expectations, how would you rate us on the following categories?

_____ Service, responsiveness to your inquiries
Are you aware of any outstanding service issues?

_____ Communication, frequency of contact
Should we be in more, less or about the same amount of contact?

Chapter 8:

Success Habits: The Art of the Handwritten Note

This Chapter's success habit reminds you of the importance of delivering personal attention to your top clients through the use of handwritten notes. In today's world of emails, tweeting, and texting, almost everybody enjoys receiving a personal card or letter. This activity is central to delivering world-class service and can be easily accomplished with a little preparation and planning.

Reading

In today's world of emails, texting and tweeting, almost everybody appreciates a handwritten card or letter. This is particularly true of high net-worth clients who are bombarded by your competition and the financial press with offers of quick fixes or elaborate wealth planning techniques, for problems they may not even have. Therefore, a "must-do" success habit and important client communication strategy is being sure your top relationships are receiving a personal note, card, or letter at least once a quarter.

Bite-sized Pieces

Though this may sound like a difficult task, it isn't, when you turn it into a success habit, breaking down the work into manageable pieces. For example, if you have 120 clients who qualify for this level of attention and there are 60 working days in the quarter, you would need to commit to 2 correspondences per day. Taking it a step further, 180 clients would require creating 3 personal communiqués per day, and so on.

Simply put – is your business worth investing the time to write a couple of notes per day? Do your best clients deserve this level of individual attention?

You Probably Have a Head Start

When you consider birthdays, holidays, and other special events, some of your efforts to provide personal attention may already be a part of your practice. You may only need to decide how many "other" personal touches you'd like to make via handwritten correspondence each year.

Again, I'd suggest planning for a minimum of four. Your annual routine might include these fundamental ideas:

- a birthday card with a private note
- a personalized holiday card – you decide which holiday
- a "Thank you for your business and loyalty" letter
- a letter or card that's topical – investment, tax, or financial planning – or news-related, with a magazine or newspaper clipping

Add to these four basic communications the spontaneous notes you should send when you:

- have had an important meeting with a client, to thank them for their time
- learn of a client's promotion, company recognition, or new job
- take notice of an industry, company, professional, or social occurrence that impacts one or more of your clients
- hear of a birth or wedding in a client's family – children, grandchildren, etc.
- discover anything that's important to your clients for which they should be recognized, congratulated, or even consoled

Once you've done this, you're well on your way to delivering one of the critical facets of world-class client service.

So – how do you get started on this important success habit? Here's a 5-step process:

1. Determine which of your clients will be included in this effort; these may only be those you've designated as your ultimate clients. Lower-tier clients could be included, but with a decreased frequency of personal notes.
2. Print a checklist of these clients and keep it on your desk, to monitor progress.
3. You may also choose to include an extra column listing your clients' birthdates, and order your list by these dates, to be sure you send timely birthday greetings.
4. Divide the number of clients from step 1 by the number of days each quarter you anticipate sending notes; this will represent the target for your daily success habit.

5. Set aside 10 to 20 minutes each day, in order to write your notes or letters – whenever you have extra time, draft extra notes, to keep ahead of schedule.

Finally, here are a few other suggestions you may find helpful:

1. Purchase a supply of professionally-produced blank cards, to be sure you always have them available.

2. Keep a file with newspaper and magazine articles which contain relevant articles for your niche markets, as well as important investment or financial planning issues.

3. Whenever you hear good news about your clients, send them a note right away – don't put it off.

4. Consider developing quarterly themes for your notes and letters – this will allow you to develop consistent themes and it will keep you from struggling for new ideas in your day-to-day note writing.

5. Don't fake it – technology is great, but it can't replace a personal note that's written with purpose and sincerity.

6. Be brief – an old rule of thumb says you should write long letters to people you don't know (prospective clients) and short letters to those you already know (clients).

Remember, success habits are recurring activities you put in place in your business, to build for long-term success. Sending your top clients a quarterly note or letter that's highly personalized will go a long way toward greater loyalty and increased business opportunities. When you break this task down into bite-sized pieces, it's more enjoyable and easier to accomplish. *Why not get started right away?*

Chapter 9:

Quick Campaigns: Tax Reviews that Breed Client Loyalty and Convert Prospects

With the combined thoughts of differentiating your practice and the importance of tax planning, in this chapter, we bring you a campaign to help you convert your active prospects into clients. This concept may also be useful if you're looking for a tool to update your client profiles or to simply provide a value-added service to your existing clientele. If you put these ideas to work, you'll reap the rewards of stronger client relations, converting some of your active prospects into new clients – and a jump in your revenues – as you enter the final quarter of the year. Give it a try and let us know how it works!

Reading

> "The hardest thing to understand in the world is the income tax."
>
> —Albert Einstein

As a financial advisor, you sometimes need to find an edge with your prospective clients – a strategy that demonstrates how your services are uniquely suited to help these future clients accomplish their goals. For example, you may be in competition with a prospect's current advisor, so your focus would be to highlight the differences in your client-management process. Alternatively, your prospect may have never before worked with a financial professional, so your aim is to highlight the value you bring to your client relationships. No matter the scenario, you should build a series of communications and activities which increasingly display your ability to help your future clients achieve a wide range of personal and financial goals.

One of the most complex issues facing almost all clients and prospects is taxation. And, though tax advice may not necessarily be in the domain of your services as a financial advisor, it's often incidental to your wealth management, financial planning, and investment recommendations. Therefore, it's critical for your prospective clients to understand how you'll help them monitor, manage, and minimize their taxes. From income to estate tax planning, your work with a client and their tax advisor will allow them to preserve wealth and to more readily meet their long-term objectives.

With the combined thoughts of differentiating your practice and tax planning in mind, we bring you a campaign to help you convert your active prospects into clients. This concept may also be useful if you're looking for a tool to update your client profiles or to simply to provide a value-added service to your existing clientele. In general terms, we want to assist you in uncovering new business opportunities with your clients and prospects by getting them to review where they stand, tax-wise, for the current financial year.

The "10 Questions for End-of-Year Tax Planning" questionnaire we've developed and present in this chapter isn't meant to be a formal document; it's intentionally written as a series of friendly questions your clients or prospects will ask themselves. As they work through these questions, they'll probably find they need your help, allowing you to spend time creating or building relationships and new business. You should then uncover asset capture, cross-selling and new account opportunities which will add to your commissions and fees. Although this campaign could be conducted exclusively through the mail, for greatest effect, you may choose to follow up by telephone, and schedule appointments where appropriate.

To some, the timing of this "tax awareness" concept may seem out of sync with a traditional tax-planning calendar, but we find this to be an ideal, important time of year to encourage this review and update. First, you're able to more easily help your clients execute investment strategies requiring doubling positions or selling positions that are tied to 31-day waiting periods for completion and current tax year recognition. Second, if your clients own businesses or have flexible corporate retirement plans, there may be opportunities to capture additional tax deferral, if they act before calendar-year end. Third, you avoid the "I have until April" syndrome, as well as minimize the last-minute and sometimes-frantic decisions made during the waning days of December. Finally – and most important – you distinguish yourself as a financial professional who is constantly on the lookout to provide value-added service with your clients' best interests at heart.

Active Prospect Campaign Steps

1. Create a list of your best active prospects – those with whom you've made several contacts and are convinced would be good clients for your practice. You might think of these folks as being difficult to "close," and you're looking for an added edge, to convince them to establish a new relationship.

2. Mail each person on your list the "Active Prospect Tax Planning Letter" and the "10 Questions for End-of-Year Tax Planning" we've provided in this book. You may choose to adjust this letter to fit your business style, though it's intentionally written to be friendly, so as not to come across as being "canned."

3. Follow each letter up with a telephone call within five business days, to be sure your prospect has received it or to emphasize the importance of this planning review, and to look for opportunities to discuss new business.

4. Where appropriate, you should schedule more formal appointments for investment, wealth, or financial planning discussions. These meetings could be excellent times to review your client-management process and to utilize your conceptual selling skills.

5. Special considerations:

   • If you're not a professional tax planner, be sure to reference the need to include the prospect's tax planner. Do *not* give tax advice if you aren't licensed to do so!

   • If you have a large active prospect database, mail these letters in manageable groups, so as not to get behind on follow-up calls or be overwhelmed by incoming calls and questions.

- You may choose to be less selective, in terms of which prospects receive this letter and questionnaire – just remember that the quality of prospects who participate in this campaign will be proportionate to your success. Keep your definition of an ideal client and your niche markets in mind when you build your list.

- If you have a sales or service assistant, you could easily create a script, allowing them to conduct the follow-up calls. Their goal would be to uncover prospects with greatest need for immediate help and to schedule telephone or in-person appointments for you.

Client Campaign Steps

1. Develop a list of clients who you believe would benefit from this campaign; they'll more than likely come from your "B" and "C" client segments. Though all your clients should complete a year-end tax review, the letter in this version of the campaign is aimed at helping you uncover opportunities with clients who may not yet fall into your ideal client status.

2. Your "A" clients – those with whom you work the closet – might find this process or the letter to be too formal. If you like the questionnaire and believe it would add value to your top client relationships, simply send it with a handwritten note or personal letter that acknowledges the work you've already done on their behalf on some of these tax issues during the year.

3. Mail the "Fourth Quarter Client Tax Planning Letter" and the "10 Questions for End-of-Year Tax Planning." You may choose to adjust these to fit your business style, though they're intentionally written to be friendly, so as not to come across as being "canned."

4. Follow each letter up with a telephone call – within five business days – to be sure your client has received it, to emphasize the importance of this planning review, and to look for opportunities to discuss new business opportunities.

5. Where appropriate, you should schedule more formal appointments for investment, wealth, or financial planning discussions.

6. Special considerations:

   • If you aren't a professional tax planner, be sure to reference the need to include the client's tax planner. Do *not* give tax advice if you aren't licensed to do so!

   • If you have a large client database, mail these letters in manageable groups, so as not to get behind on follow-up calls and to avoid being overwhelmed by incoming calls and questions.

   • If you have a sales or service assistant, you could easily create a script, allowing them to conduct the follow-up calls. Their goal would be to uncover clients with the greatest need for immediate help, and schedule telephone or in-person appointments for you.

There you have it: two campaigns which demonstrate the value-added services you bring to your client relationships and simultaneously help your clients and prospects conduct critical year-end tax reviews. It can be used any time with prospects and is most useful for your clients when you conduct a campaign in the fourth quarter of the year. You'll reap the rewards of stronger client relations, conversion of your active prospects into new clients, and see a jump in your commissions and fees as you enter the final quarter of the year. *Give it a try and let us know how it works!*

Active Prospect Tax Planning Letter

Dear <*active prospect name*>,

> *"The hardest thing to understand in the world is the income tax."*
>
> *Albert Einstein*

Many of us feel just like Albert Einstein when it comes to taxes. From filing deadlines, to keeping good records, to rule changes, thoughts of paying taxes aren't just relegated to the end of the year or to April 15th. And – though we recognize this letter may seem out of season – we know spending time over the next 30 days doing a quick tax assessment may position you to minimize your taxes for the current financial year.

Over the years, we've found that many tax savings opportunities are missed because tax planning is put off until it's too late to make a difference. Many financial advisors don't let their clients know there are decisions they can make today that may not be available in December or next April. In fact, in our client work, we're currently conducting personal investment and financial planning reviews with a focus on uncovering tax saving strategies. Once we identify potential opportunities, we work with our clients and their tax professionals to implement changes.

As someone we would very much like to have as a client of our practice, we would like to offer you a similar opportunity. Enclosed with this letter is a copy of the "10 Questions for End-of-Year Tax Planning" we use during our client meetings. Please look the questions over and let us know if you'd like to discuss them, either in-person or over the phone. If not, we at least hope you find it useful as you complete your own tax update.

The choice of how you undertake this review is up to you – most importantly, please don't put it off until it's too late to make a difference. Working together with a professional financial advisor and your tax professional, you may find more choices for tax savings than you previously thought existed. We would simply like to help!

None of us may have the total brainpower of Albert Einstein but, when it comes to taxes, we can all be just as smart, if we do a little advance planning. Remember – Albert Einstein also defined insanity as, "doing the same thing over and over again and expecting different results."

All the best,

<your name>

P.S.: If you think our "10 Questions for End-of-Year Tax Planning" would benefit one of your friends or relatives, please let us know and we will send them a copy.

Fourth Quarter Client Tax Planning Letter

Dear <client name>,

> *"The hardest thing to understand in the world is the income tax."*
>
> *Albert Einstein*

Many of us feel just like Albert Einstein when it comes to taxes. What's more, from extended filing deadlines, to good record keeping, to rule changes, thoughts of paying taxes are not just relegated to the end of the year or to April 15th. And – though we recognize this letter may seem out of season – we know spending time over the next 30 days doing a quick tax assessment may position you to minimize your taxes for the current financial year.

Over the years, we've found that many tax savings opportunities are missed because tax planning is put off until it's too late to make a difference. There are choices to be made at this time of year that may not be available in December or next April. To help you consider these decisions, we have enclosed a copy of our "10 Questions for End-of-Year Tax Planning."

Please look these 10 questions over and let us know if you'd like to discuss them further, either in-person or over the phone. Of course, we would consult with your accountant before making any decisions or implementing any changes. We hope that, in working together, we may find more choices for tax savings than you previously thought existed.

None of us may have the total brainpower of Albert Einstein but, when it comes to taxes, we can all be just as smart, if we do a little advance planning. Remember – Albert Einstein also defined insanity as, "doing the same thing over and over again and expecting different results."

All the best,

<your name>

P.S. If you think our "10 Questions for End-of-Year Tax Planning" would benefit one of your friends or relatives, please let us know and we will send them a copy.

10 Questions for End-of-Year Tax Planning

This worksheet is designed with simple questions aimed at helping you assess your current and projected tax situation. Begin by taking notes and highlighting areas that may require further investigation and clarification. We'll review this questionnaire during our review meeting. As appropriate, we'll consult with your tax advisor, before making any final decisions.

General Income Planning: Consider your salary, bonuses, retirement plan payouts, job changes, or any other events that may have important financial implications:

Will my taxable income in the current financial year be significantly higher than it was in the previous financial year? If so, have I had the proper amount of taxes withheld or made quarterly payments that will allow me to avoid potential underpayment penalties?

I expect my income to be lower next year. Is there a way to defer earned income into future years? Also consider the reverse scenario of taking more income this year.

Investment Planning: Review how your investments have performed so far this year and consider any significant taxable events that may occur between now and the end of the year.

So far this year, are my capital gains higher or lower than they were in the previous financial year? Do I hold any investments that, if sold, could generate capital losses to offset gains or, potentially, ordinary income? For investments, I prefer to hold for the long-term – have I considered tax-swapping strategies for realizing capital losses?

Do I own any mutual funds, partnerships, or hedge funds that may make "surprise" taxable distributions before year-end? If so, do any opportunities exist to avoid or defer these distributions?

Retirement Plans and Planning: The rules for making IRA and retirement plan contributions and distributions for individuals and businesses have changed numerous times over the past few years. You should be sure you understand these changes and how they affect your current and future taxes.

Am I maximizing my company and personal retirement planning options for deferring income and growing my nest egg? Am I taking maximum advantage of the company match in my 401k plan? Which is better for me – a Roth or traditional IRA? What are my contribution limits? Am I entitled to any "catch-up" opportunities for making contributions to any of these plans?

I am older than age 70 1/2 and have to take Required Minimum Distributions (RMD) from my IRAs – What's the deadline for taking my distribution? How much will it be this year? Should I take more than the minimum? What's the benefit to consolidating my IRAs?

I am self-employed or work in a small company: Are there retirement savings plans designed specifically for me? Will they allow me to defer greater amounts of income than traditional plans?

Gifting, Education Planning, and Charitable Contributions: A final area for review falls under the general concept of "gifting." From educational savings plans, to outright gifts, to charitable contributions, there may be strategies that will allow you to accomplish personal goals while reducing your tax burden.

From a tax-planning perspective, is there a more efficient method for funding my children's – or grandchildren's or other dependents' – educational needs? Should I review or update my 529 plans, custodial accounts, or educational IRAs? I am/my spouse is considering pursuing a new degree – are there tax strategies for advanced funding?

I understand there are annual limitations on the value of gifts I may make to any one individual – what is that limit? Are there advantages to maximizing gifts to certain family members? My children are financially secure – are there tax-advantaged strategies for making gifts to my grandchildren?

I am charitably inclined – is it better to gift cash or appreciated securities to my favorite charities? I don't have a favorite charity at this time and have heard about personal foundations and gift funds – how do these work? I own a highly-appreciated stock I would never sell, because of the taxes, but could use some additional income – how do charitable trusts work?

Chapter 10:

A Client Communication Strategy: Simplicity & Consistency for Increased Results

> Many client-communication success stories have two common themes: consistency and simplicity. With this in mind, this chapter is a refresher course on a simple and highly effective client communication process.

"Everything should be made as simple as possible, but not simpler."

—*Albert Einstein*

Reading

In a recent conversation with a top producer, we discussed the topic of client communication and how to get the most out of every relationship. We weren't talking about pushing products but, rather, how to be sure you're truly the primary advisor to your best clients. We agreed this was a topic many advisors either take for granted or over-complicate – an interesting dichotomy. He then went on to explain his process for continuously growing his production by double digits with a simple client contact system – and *no* prospecting.

Intrigued by this discussion, I decided to speak with a few more top producers and to look back at some recent client communication success stories, to see if there were any common themes. I found two: consistency and simplicity. This strategy has worked for the 20 years I've been in this industry and probably long before.

Setting the Stage

The goal of this communication strategy is to create a systematic approach for calling all your clients, based on their importance to your practice. You'll be utilizing pro-active calling with a simple letter or email to those you don't reach. When combined with client meetings, regular correspondence, and the interactions of daily business, you'll build loyalty and increase production.

While on the surface this approach may seem to require an inordinate number of phone calls, your focal point should be implementing the process – not the actual number of clients you contact on a monthly basis. Over time, the discipline of the process will have a dramatic effect on your practice. From business you uncover on your outgoing calls, to clients calling back when they receive your letter or when they need investment help, you've all but guaranteed you're their advisor of choice.

"But I Don't Have a Transaction-Oriented Business."

The concept of having a regular telephoning strategy sometimes falls on deaf ears for those who have planning or investment management-oriented practices. It may appear unprofessional or unnecessary, given the nature of client relationships in these business models. Two thoughts: 1) This strategy is proven to work in all business models. 2) We've never heard of clients complaining about too much service. Keep reading and see what you think. Better yet, give it a try for a few months and see if it improves your results.

Step 1: Get prepared – Your first step should be to produce a list of all your clients – nothing fancy. Print an alphabetical listing of your client relationships – not accounts – including addresses, phone numbers, and a blank column, for use in the next step. Depending on how you manage your database, this should take no more than 10 to 20 minutes.

Step 2: A, B, C Segments – Next, you need to decide, if you haven't already, which of your clients should be contacted monthly, quarterly, or annually. This doesn't have to be scientific – it's a simple A, B, C strategy, based on your perception of the value of each relationship. Reflect on current business, potential business, referrals, and your instincts. If you aren't sure, err on the side of more contacts – you can always adjust the segments later. Just shut your office door – you may want to include your assistant – and place an A (monthly), B (quarterly), or C (annually) in the blank column on your calling list. Don't over-think it and you'll be done in less than an hour.

Step 3: Build Call Lists – Based on your segments above, construct three lists that contain the same information as your original list. If you printed your first list through a spreadsheet download, you could simply do a sort, based on the A, B, C column, and it'll only take a few minutes. On the other hand, if your process is more manual, it may take a bit more time – but, having three lists is essential. By the way, if your contact management system has fields in which you can record your segments, go ahead and take the time to do it. Once you see how powerful this idea can be, you'll want to conduct this strategy monthly, and being able to quickly generate your three lists will make it easier.

Step 4: Decide on a script – Although you could certainly use this monthly opportunity to introduce a new idea, product, or service, it's not crucial. Your script can simply let your clients know you're checking in to say "hello" and see if they have any questions.

Step 5: Get on the phone – You – and your team – are now ready to start making calls. Your goal is not necessarily to speak with every client on your list. Your focus should be on the discipline of systematically working through your lists, as outlined below. You won't converse with each client you call, but you will have a follow-up system for letting them know you tried. The combination of calls and follow-up to those you miss demonstrates your commitment to staying in regular contact, through good times and bad, and it proves you're constantly striving to be their primary advisor.

Step 6: Follow-up for those you miss – We cannot stress this point enough – you should *not* leave messages for clients to call back. Mark them on your call sheet for your follow-up letter or email. When you get an answering machine or voicemail, simply hang up. If you speak with an assistant or receptionist, you'll need to identify yourself – but don't leave a callback message, if your client is unavailable.

The follow-up itself is a very short letter or email that lets your client know you tried to call to say "hello," and they can call you back, if they have questions, need help, or just want to review their investments. If your clients are frequent users of email, we strongly suggest this alternative. You can use the same text in your letter each and every month, because what the letter says is not nearly as important as the discipline of the activity. Alternatively, some months, you may have a new idea to introduce, or news to share and it's perfectly acceptable to include this information with your standard letter.

Call Your "A" Clients Monthly

Set aside time each day to contact those clients you've chosen for monthly calls. We suggest at least one hour per day, plus any open time slots you may have, between meetings and other activities. Start at the beginning of the alphabet and try to get through your entire "A" list during the first two weeks of the month. Don't worry if you don't finish – keep going until you've completed your list.

Again, you shouldn't leave messages for clients to call back – mark them on your call sheet for your follow-up letter or email. When you get an answering machine or voicemail, simply hang up. If you speak with an assistant or receptionist, you'll need to identify yourself, but don't leave a callback message, if your client is unavailable.

Divide Your "B" Clients into Thirds

Your "B" clients are those whom you've decided to call quarterly. Divide this alphabetical list by three and call one-third of the list each month, after you've completed your "A" list. Ideally, this will be in the third week of the month and you'll finish by the end of the week.

If not and you have time, keep going. Alternatively, start this list where you left off when you get back to your "B" clients the following month. Use the same rule as with "A" clients – no need to leave messages.

Split Your "C" Clients into 12 Groups

For reasons of your own choosing, you've decided these clients only get one outgoing call per year. Dividing them into 12 groups helps you organize this task. After you finish with your monthly "A" and "B" client calls, move to this group. If you run out of time, continue down the list next month, starting where you finished during the current month. No need to leave messages.

Your Assistant or Team Can Help

Depending on the structure of your team and the size of your book, you may want to involve others in this calling process. Although you should reserve the "A" client calls for yourself or a senior partner, the remaining two segments could be called by a sales, marketing, or service assistant. Remember, the key to your success is the process of attempting to call all scheduled clients each month.

Consider Some Simple Math

You may think making this many calls sounds impossible. Let's look at a fairly typical example. If you have 500 client relationships, statistically speaking, approximately 20% are "A" clients – about 100. To call 100 clients over the first two weeks of the month – 10 business days – is only 10 calls per day. When you consider you may only get through to half these folks – five per day – it doesn't seem like an overwhelming task. Don't forget – these are your best clients;

regardless of this strategy, you probably need to speak with many of them at some point in the month anyway.

If you break the remaining clients evenly into two groups of 200, you'll have 67 "B" clients (200 divided by 3) and 17 "C" clients (200 divided by 12) to call each month. This is a total of 84 divided by the remaining 10 business days in the month, or about 8 calls per day – very manageable. If this process is shared with or given to an assistant, you could move through an entire cycle during the first two weeks of the month.

To keep up with this strategy, you and your team are making just 10 client calls per day and, on a typical day, speaking with about half those clients. Most successful practices more than double this number of calls and contacts, so this gives you a solid baseline, with plenty of time for more specific calls and meetings with clients and prospects.

What Should You Expect?

The best way to think about potential results is to expect the unexpected. Some of the people you'll talk to will have immediate needs that mean immediate new business. Other conversations will lead to uncovering service issues that help you maintain your client service standards, thus keeping small concerns from becoming big ones. You may just brighten the day of one of your clients. The possibilities are endless.

The biggest surprises will probably come when you don't speak with a client. Your systematic approach to client communication leads them to call you when they have a financial planning or investment need you may not have previously discussed. As their 'primary advisor,' you get the call to invest the unplanned-for bonus or inheritance, review the estate plan, or help with the rollover.

We know some who are reading this Chapter believe they'll get these calls without this process, and you may be right. But, when investors are surveyed, they tell us they tend to speak with the last person who contacted them – this system helps you be that person each and every month. We also know many advisors struggle on a month-to-month basis to find a new campaign or idea for growing business – this strategy gives you a strong foundation. Give it a try – it has worked and continues to work well for many top producers.

We started this chapter with a quote from Albert Einstein: *"Everything should be made as simple as possible, but not simpler."* If you're looking for a simple strategy to improve your client communication process and grow production along the way, give this strategy a try for a few months and you'll probably become hooked. The only way to make it simpler – which Albert Einstein advises against – is not to have a system for contacting your clients. In either case, the results will speak for themselves.

Financial Advisor Telephone Script

"Hello, <Mr./Ms./Mrs. client>…"

"This is <your name> at <your firm>."

"I'm calling just to say 'hello' and see if any questions have come up since we last spoke. You may have received a statement, seen something on the news, or just come across an idea you'd like to discuss."

<Pause and wait for a response. Discuss whatever the client mentions – listen and be attentive, so as not to appear to be just going through the motions.>

<If there is no specific topic, here are four options>:

1. "How have you and your family been?" <be as personal as possible>

2. Tell a story about something that's done well in the client's portfolio or a success you've had in working with another client.

3. Bring up something that's been in the news or relates to the industry and ask the client for their opinion or reaction.

4. "By the way, we've been working on <new idea> with some of our other clients. <Mention a specific benefit>. Would you like to hear about it, too?"

<Thank client for their time and end call. Don't forget to follow up on issues the client has brought to your attention.>

Assistant Telephone Script

"Hello, <Mr./Ms./Mrs. client>..."

"This is <your name> at <your firm>. <your advisor> asked me to call you."

"<your advisor> just wanted to be sure we touched base, to say 'hello' and see if any questions have come up since we last spoke. You may have received a statement, seen something on the news, or just come across an idea you'd like to discuss."

<Pause and wait for a response. Discuss whatever the client mentions – listen and be attentive, so as not to appear to be just going through the

motions. Be on the lookout for opportunities for new business, or for service improvement that may require scheduling follow-up for your advisor.>

<If there's no specific topic, here are four options>:

1. "To be sure we're in touch when you need our help, is there anything we should be looking for? Perhaps you have some funds coming available or you'd like us to update your financial plan."

2. "By the way, we've been working on *<new idea>* with some of our other clients. *<Mention a specific benefit>* Would you like to hear about it, too?" *<If yes, either pass the call through to your advisor or, if more appropriate, schedule time for your advisor to call back.>*

<Thank client for their time, and end call. Don't forget to follow up on issues the client has brought to your attention.>

Follow-up Letter or Email

Send this letter or email when your client isn't available to take your call – don't leave messages.

Remember, it's possible to use the same letter each month. If you have an idea or news item you'd like to put in front of your clients, it could be included with this correspondence.

Dear *<client name – be sure to personalize>*,

I hope this letter finds you well. I tried to call today to say 'hello' and see if there is any way we can be of service. There's no need for you to return my call, but please let me know if you have questions about your most recent statements, specific investment ideas, or anything you may have come across in the news that's causing concern. I enjoy our relationship and am available even if you'd just like to talk or share a story.

<Optional:> By the way, I've enclosed *<an investment idea, a news story, a financial planning update>* that you might find interesting. Please call me if it sparks any questions.

As always, I'll call again this time next *<month, quarter, year>*.

All the best,
<personalized signature>

<optional: – if you want to collect your clients' email addresses for future correspondence – P.S. Many of my clients are finding that email is a good way to stay in regular contact. If you have an email address that I could use from time to time, to inform you of new developments, please email me at *<your email address>* and I'll save your address in my files. I promise not to abuse the privilege and will only use it when appropriate.

Chapter 11:
More Client Contact Equals Increased Income

In this chapter, we'll review brief success and frustration statements and point to resources that will help you achieve improved activity results. We premise this information on the fact that an activity-based plan which focuses on maximizing time spent with clients and prospects will *always* lead to increases in financial advisor income. It's when we get way from this simple strategy that business stagnates or falls.

"Good will plus good service brings sales success that no competition can possibly undersell."

—*Harry F. Banks*

Reading

As part of our coaching efforts, we published a series of articles we grouped as "activity tests." Our goal was to challenge our readers to keep an eye on their activities for eight weeks, in order to measure how much time they were actually spending in client- and prospect-facing activities. We know from experience – and the many studies that have been done in recent years – the more time you spend with clients, the more your income will grow. Equally important, your clients will be happier and in a better position to accomplish their financial goals.

You may have been part of this "challenge." While we don't know how each of you has fared during this challenge, or even if you've participated at all, we want to share several examples of activity success and suggest why these results were achieved. Read through these simple scenarios and consider how they might apply to your practice.

> *"I knew I didn't have all of my clients' assets but, by focusing on spending more time with my top clients, I found many surprises. One client in particular was not worth the three million dollars listed in my records – he was worth ten million dollars and wasn't happy with his other advisors."*

This is typical of the most frequent and significant results we hear from advisors who re-focus their efforts on increasing the amount of time they spend with their clients. All too often, we allow ourselves to get caught up in the minutiae of our business, or we turn ourselves into analysts and researchers and forget the single most important asset we have is our client relationships. The best way to take care of this asset is to spend the vast majority of your time talking, meeting, writing, thanking, or communicating in any other way possible with your clients. Your income and your satisfaction with your work will grow proportionately.

> *"I honestly don't have enough clients and prospects to keep me busy. I get so caught up with handling service issues that are more appropriate for my assistant, debating the news of the day, and dealing with some smaller clients who take up*

an inordinate amount of time, so the important stuff is being neglected. My best clients don't hear from me enough – in fact, I don't have enough best clients, and my prospect database is so old I feel like I have to start all over again."

This is certainly a mouthful but, again, it resembles some of the common frustrations of advisors who don't take proactive control of their daily activities. We all sometimes get so busy being busy we get swallowed up in other people's priorities. Over time, for financial advisors, this 'busyness' can lead to a practice with too few good clients and too few solid prospects. Production ends up stagnating or dropping – the advisor is truly in a position of not having enough people to contact. The best way to rectify this condition is to develop a client and prospect management system that begins with proper segmentation and is maintained with a disciplined communication schedule. This can give the advisor the upper hand – an activity-based plan that's biased toward maximizing time spent where it counts – with clients and prospects.

"My increased focus on activity-based planning has led to a big increase in referrals. Instead of just randomly asking for referrals and not counting how often I did it, one of my activities now is to count the number of times I mention referrals. I actually set a weekly goal to challenge myself. It's not that I've gotten better with how I ask, I'm just doing it more consistently, with incredible results."

Whether you're trying to increase referrals, cross-sell a new service, uncover new assets, open accounts or achieve any of a number of other possible goals, the best way to start is by first making a commitment to activity. Do you need more referrals? Make sure you're asking for or promoting them ten times a week. Would you like to determine if your investment clients have established a solid estate plan? Call five of them each week – that's just one per day – and quickly explain the service you offer and why it's important. Not all your clients will have an interest – but your activity will ultimately result in new business opportunities. On top of this, an even greater number of your clients will have an added appreciation for the work you do and will be grateful for you going the extra mile. The examples are endless – but they all begin with establishing a plan for an activity predicated on spending more time with clients and prospective clients.

You can take the challenge yourself by visiting the Encore Library (www.EncorePartners.com/UCEbook).

Don't forget – we're always looking for more financial advisor successes stories. Please email us at robb@encorepartners.com if you'd like to share your results.

Chapter 12:

Client Advocacy Short Course: Quickly Create a Stream of High-Quality Referrals

> Client advocacy tops our list of effective methods for capturing high-quality referrals. Based on our popular DVD program, this chapter walks you through our advocacy "short course" and delivers a clear-cut process for making advocacy a part of your regular client interactions. What's more, you can put this idea to work today!

Reading

Client advocacy is a process for strengthening relationships and building a steady stream of high-quality referrals. Many advisors miss out on this proven technique because they're not sure how to adapt it to their current way of doing business. This short course details a simple strategy for making advocacy a part of your regular routine. The concept of building client advocacy to gain referrals has gained a good deal of momentum among our Encore Partners, Online Solutions, and advanced mentoring clients. With this in mind, we were asked to create a short course – a quick overview of the advocacy process presented in more detail earlier in this book – demonstrating the way you might use it on a short-term basis in your daily or weekly activities. While this might be a review for some of you, for others, it may give you the impetus you need to make advocacy a part of your business. As always, we'll give you an actionable idea you can put to work right away. The benefits are that you'll gain a simple process for growing your practice, you'll learn how to build a pipeline of high-quality referrals, and, at the same time, you'll develop stronger relationships with your best clients.

Let's start by considering the sources of new client relationships. More specifically, how do you uncover your best new relationships? When I ask this question of financial advisors, they most often tell me their best new relationships come from referrals. This is substantiated by many studies. Most new client relationships are coming from referrals – something in the neighborhood of 90%. Fewer than 10% of clients are coming from direct marketing and other sources. The time-consuming expensive stuff only puts a small dent in your client acquisition success. The feeling you may have – that your best relationships are coming from referrals – is backed up by facts! So – if you're looking for a way to bring new, significant relationships into your practice, an active advocacy process is an important consideration.

You may be thinking, "You know – I get referrals!" However, I have to ask: Are you receiving *enough* referrals? Can you count on them?

When you build advocacy into your business, referrals become a regular part of what you do. Referrals are dependable – you control the stream of referrals you receive. There are many challenges to uncovering referrals – there's the fear of pushing too hard, not wanting to appear unprofessional. There's a debate: should I directly ask for referrals or just promote them by telling people I accept new clients? Either way, you have to do it regularly.

What about timing? When is the right time to ask for referrals or to promote referrals? We've all faced that uncomfortable blank stare, asking for that referral, only to have a client look us in the eye and say, "You know – I really don't know who to talk with you about!" Or, we've had clients just throw out a name at random that isn't carefully thought through. Also, if you *are* receiving referrals on a regular basis, are they qualified – are you properly introduced so you can easily close them, so those people will easily become clients of your practice?

Let's move forward and get into the advocacy process as a way of making sure you're not only receiving referrals, but also making sure you're getting *enough* referrals for the type of growth that you want to build into your business.

I define an advocate as a person – or a group of people – who have an almost inexplicable desire to see you and your practice succeed. They're promoters; they're campaigners; they're supporters. We all have them. Sometimes, they're good clients, sometimes they're family members or friends, or social acquaintances, or other professionals. Yet, they're people who are really looking out for us, and they really are doing it for no other reason than they want to see us succeed. We all have advocates, and we can all build more advocates into our practice – if we talk to our clients about the mutual benefits of advocacy.

I believe advocacy is one the most effective methods of growing your practice. It helps you stay in touch with your target markets because, when you're talking with your clients about advocacy, they're generally going to refer you to people who are similar to themselves – people who are in your target markets. You take control of the referral process – you're not just waiting for referrals to happen. You can actually cut down on a lot of wasted prospecting, because you can grow your business without sacrificing more time and more effort.

Finally, advocacy helps you build stronger relationships with your existing clients. When you let your clients know you consider them to be advocates, they'll see more than just the benefit to you in the growth of your business through the referrals they give you. They'll also see the benefit to them – because, as advocates of your practice and as people you view as ideal clients, they're getting better service in return. The more they can help you, the more you can help them. By their giving you referrals, they're freeing up your time. By giving you referrals to people who are similar to themselves, you have more time to deal with the type of people they are, allowing you to develop greater expertise. Advocacy is a two-way street. That's why I think it's one of the most effective methods of growing your practice.

Over the years, I've heard several great advocacy success stories, but one sticks out, in particular. An advisor with whom I was consulting was working with a client who was employed by a major telephone company. This advisor specialized in 401k plans, so he took the time to look at the client's retirement plan document, to see if in-service withdrawals were a possibility. They were – and he landed a great IRA rollover account to really help this client work more specifically on his retirement goals in a more professional fashion. He wanted to find more people in a situation similar to his client's so, instead of just blankly asking his client, "Who do you know in the company that might have rollover money?" he did a little homework. He went to a cross-reference directory, where he was able to uncover the names of several other people who worked for this company who he felt his client might know. When he mentioned their names, he got a lot of great feedback – not just feedback as to whether or not the folks he mentioned would be good clients, but also feedback as to other people who were in similar situations. By specifically mentioning the names of people, this advisor felt he engaged the client in a conversation that made it much easier for him to consider who would be a good referral and who wouldn't be a good referral. This landed the advisor several more very large IRA rollover accounts – money he thought he couldn't get his hands on. I bet you all have situations just like this – situations where you know a client, you know who they know, and you just need to find out a way to get introduced to those people they know, to find out for sure if they'll be good clients for your practice.

If that success story and the other ideas I discussed earlier have you intrigued, then I'd really like to help you get started on advocacy today. To do this, I want you to walk you through a series of five questions:

1. Which of your clients are on your calendar this week and the next?
2. What do you know about them? What are their interests?
3. Who do you think they know?
4. Do they understand the benefits of advocacy? Have you talked to them about advocacy before?
5. Do you have time to meet with highly-qualified prospects over the next 30 to 60 days? I bet you do.

Which of your clients are on your calendar this week and the next?

I want to help you understand how you can work with the people you're already going to meet this week and next, to talk about advocacy and start building referrals right away. In the worksheet below, this reading material is a blank matrix. This will give you an opportunity to do a little bit of homework around the people you already have appointments with. These could be in-person appointments or telephone appointments. Very quickly – in the first column – write down the names of the people you're getting ready to meet with.

What do you know about them? What are their interests?

It should only take you a couple of minutes more to think: how did they become clients of your practice? How do you know them? Next, in the third column – column C – list their occupations. This might take you a little more time – you may have to look in your contact management system or get your assistant to help you, but write down the names of their occupations. Fourth, what else do you know about them – what organizations do they belong to, what interests do they have? List this information in column D. This will help you do a little research in advance of your meeting.

Who do you think they know?

Once you've made your list of the clients you're going to be meeting with this week and what their interests are, by completing column B, C, and D, it's time to do a little brainstorming – considering who you think they might know. For example, let's say you have a client named Nancy Davies. In column B, next to Nancy Davies, you can see that you know her personally through a charity board. Nancy, because of her involvement in that charity board, knows other charity board members. Could they be potential referrals to your practice? Could Nancy give you an introduction?

As I mentioned earlier, the goal of creating this short course on advocacy is to tie the advocacy process to daily and weekly activities you're already working on. I believe, if you take an extra 10 or 15 minutes as preparation for your client meetings, you can easily uncover two to five prospective clients as possible references from each of the clients you've put on your list. That should be your goal. Come up with the names of two to five prospective clients you'd like to have as references from your advocates that you're already going to be meeting with this week.

To help you brainstorm, let's look at some potential sources – some places you might go to uncover those two to five names you'd like to mention to the clients with whom you're getting ready to meet. Think about organizations they might belong to – perhaps the chamber of commerce, a civic club, a country club, a hobby-related club – or, are they on the board of directors of a locally-run corporation, a charity or a small bank? Who do they know through those boards? Are they involved with charities? Are they on the board of a charity? Do they know some of the other large donors to the charity? What are their special interests – hobbies, alumni groups, their children's schools? If you're not sure, you can add an extra step to this process and, in your next meeting, ask your client advocates for some help: "What clubs do you belong to? What other things you are involved in?"

The more you know about your clients, the better off you are, and the better they feel about you, because you're taking more of a personal interest.

In doing this extra homework, spending the extra 10 minutes before the meeting to come up with these names, the Internet is your friend. You'll be amazed what you can find just by doing some free Internet searches, going to Google or LinkedIn. These tools give you the opportunity to plug in the names or general information you have about your clients' interests and uncover people they might know. You won't believe the kinds of things I've been able to uncover while helping other people, in parts of the country that I'm not even familiar with, by using only the Internet! Of course, there are also print resources: even the Yellow Pages, or the Chamber of Commerce listings can be a great place to go. Looking at board listings or annual reports can be a good way to get information about charitable organizations as well as companies. Donor guides, membership lists… all these resources are available without taking a lot of time. When you get used to the process of spending an extra 10 or 15 minutes in preparation for an important client meeting, so you can consider who your clients know, the better off you're going to be, because you're going to be able to talk about advocacy very pointedly. You're going to be able to very specifically promote referrals to your practice.

Do they understand the benefits of advocacy? Have you talked to them about advocacy before?

Of course, once you've done this homework, it's still important that you think about how you're going approach this process. Your meeting could actually take several different formats. It could be a friendly and casual lunch you already planned on having with a client, just to chat – not necessarily to talk too much about business, but you can bring up advocacy during this conversation. As I've said earlier, you can make it part of a review. It could be part of a telephone call or a telephone checkup. No matter the format of the meeting – whether it's over the phone or in person, it's important to have an agenda. And, on that agenda, make sure one of the categories that gets listed is advocacy. Under that category, list the names and interests of the people you've uncovered. You want to prove to your client that you've spent some time thinking about this. Again, be prepared with a list of two to five prospective clients. Have a bit of a script – you don't want to stumble over your words. Practice what you're going to say. Talk with your clients about the importance of advocacy, how they're an ideal client of your practice, and how one of the best ways to grow your business is to have more clients like the one you're speaking with. That's a compliment – they'll appreciate that. You can extend that by telling them how the more ideal clients you have, the more time you're able to spend with each of your ultimate clients, and the more time you're able to research issues that face clients who fall into that ultimate client grouping within your target market segment. Tell your clients that you respect their opinion – people like to be asked for their opinion – and then slowly review your list. Go over those two to five names. Take a lot of notes – be very attentive. Ask follow-up questions. What you'll find is you'll get references, not only to the two to five people you put in front of them, although not all of them, you'll also get references to unidentified names. You've placed a specific idea in the minds of your clients. You're not asking a "maybe" question – you're specifically saying, "You're an ultimate client of my practice. You know this person through the chamber board or through this charity, or through work. Do you think they'll be a good client, just like you?" That process is very powerful and, once you get used to it, it becomes very easy. You gain the type of referrals you really need to take your business to the next level.

Finally, make sure you ask permission to use your client's name when you call on the referral and make sure you find out how you can use it. Can you use it directly or indirectly? Make that clear. You don't want to upset your existing relationships by overstepping your bounds, saying something like, "You know, my client told me to call you," if they only said, "Call them and you can mention my name, but don't say that I specifically said to call." Either way, the referral will be helpful – but you don't want to abuse the permission that's been given.

Do you have time to meet with highly-qualified prospects over the next 30 to 60 days? I bet you do.

Consider these possibilities. How many client meetings do you hold each week? Five doesn't seem like a big number to me – that's one per day. What if, for the next four weeks, you committed – during each of five client meetings – to the promotion of just two references? You're going to promote a total of 40 references over the course of four weeks. If, on average, you receive one referral from each meeting you conduct, that means you're going to uncover 20 prospective clients! The averages are much higher than one out of two, but even if one out of two references that you promote garners one referral, that's still not bad – 20 prospective clients to speak with. What if, over the next 30 to 60 days, you met with those 20 prospective clients and only closed half of them – and I bet your closing ratio is higher, when you meet a qualified referral? That's 10 new appointments over 30 to 60 days, just by mentioning the advocacy process, promoting very specific referrals to the people you're already going to meet with.

The same kind of numbers play out if you just want to do it over the telephone. Make 10 calls per week for the next four weeks – just two calls a day. Promote two references during each call – that's 80 references you promote. Your average will probably be a little lower, because you're talking over the phone and not meeting in person – but, what if it's just one half of a reference per call, on average? That's 40 prospective clients that you'll uncover over a four-week period of time, just by mentioning the advocacy process in a couple of calls per day. If you only close 50% of those 40 prospective clients, that's 20 new clients. It may take you more than 30 or 60 days to meet with them all and close the business, but that gives you a good head start on this quarter, the next quarter – or the for rest of the year, for that matter. Think about the possibilities; relate these numbers to the way you run your business.

Now is the time to follow up with those references. Don't forget – and do it quickly. Don't let those leads go stale! Call for an appointment, use your reference – use your client in a way you've been given permission to use his or her name. When you meet with that prospective client, use your normal introduction presentation with an emphasis, where you can, on the advocate who brought you to that reference, but also on the advocacy process itself. This new potential client will then understand the professional way you're growing your business – through the careful selection of potential clients from good quality referrals.

Finally, don't forget to include your client-management process. Explain specifically what a relationship with you will look like – not only as a result of this meeting, but also over the long term. When you have a good formal introduction, when you conceptually introduce a relationship, you're building a strong basis for a long-term relationship and you'll quickly turn that prospective client into a client.

That's it! You're ready to improve or build advocacy into your practice today. It's as simple as thinking about the people with whom you're getting ready to meet. Recall their interests; what do you know about them and who do you think they know? Do a little bit of research in advance, taking an extra 10 or 15 minutes before an appointment to do this research. The preparation is well worth the time. Then sit down with your client. Make advocacy a part of the agenda. Talk about the mutual benefits of advocacy to you, to the client, and to the person who's been referred to you. Ask yourself: do you have the time to meet with highly-qualified prospects this week, next week, next month? Most of us do. Advocacy is a great way to get you there and cut down on your prospecting time.

Matrix 1 – Ultimate Clients Circles of Influence

A	Best Clients	B	How were they acquired?	C	Occupation	D	Interests and Organizations

Step 1: Which of your clients are on your calendar this week and next?

Use the blank matrix above:

- Column A: List the names of the clients you will be meeting or calling
- Column B: List how they were acquired (i.e. referral, cold call, seminar etc.)
- Column C: List their occupations & industries
- Column D: List at least one interest, hobby, affiliation, or organization

Step 2: What are their interests? Who do you think they know?

Using print and electronic resources – in addition to a little bit of creativity – you're ready to generate lists of future clients that fit your definition of an ultimate client. Your goal: develop a list of at least two to five prospective clients as possible references from each of your clients.

Remember:

- The best lists are free, but…
- The Internet is your friend

Clients and connection affiliations:

- Organizations (chambers of commerce, civic clubs, country clubs)
- Boards of directors (locally-run corporations, community banks)
- Charitable organizations (boards and large donors)
- Special interests (hobbies, sports, alumni groups, children's schools)
- Major local employers
- Senior citizen groups and communities
- Neighbors of top clients and prospects

Print Resources:

- Yellow Pages
- Chamber of Commerce guides
- Boards, annual reports
- Donor guides
- Membership lists

Internet Resources:

- www.google.com
- LinkedIn.com
- www.finance.yahoo.com
- www.freeerisa.com

Step 3: Do your clients understand the benefits of advocacy?

Your perspective:

An advocate is a person or group of people who have an almost inexplicable desire to see you and your practice succeed – promoter, campaigner, and supporter.

Advocate Perspective:

- Feel important
- Understand your client selection process
- More time for your clients
- Greater understanding of their unique needs

Meeting types:

- A friendly lunch
- Part of a review
- Telephone check up

Example – Client Review Meetings:

- Five meetings per week for the next four weeks
- Promote two references in each meeting (total 40)
- On average, receive one reference from each meeting

- You'll uncover 20 prospective clients
- Average new relationships: 10, if your closing ratio is only 50%

Step 4: Do you have time to meet with highly-qualified prospects?

- Conceptual selling
- Professional interview
- Review advocacy and client selectivity

Advocacy Quick Review Q&A

> Building advocacy into your practice will help you develop a steady stream of qualified referrals. This review quickly walks you through a simple five-step process for making referral-gathering a regular part of your business building routine.

Reading

Increased communication – even when you're not sure what to say – is essential to uncovering new business opportunities and delivering the service your clients deserve. One of the techniques we suggest is asking your clients the "advocacy question." Here's what we said:

> *"The advocacy question: "Do you think (your specific friend, neighbor, work associate…) would be a good fit for my practice?"*

We call this technique "building advocacy"; it's a powerful referral strategy. Simply call your clients, mention to each the specific name of someone they know personally or professionally, and ask if that person would fit in well with the way you run your practice. Obviously, before you call, you'll need to take some time to research the neighborhoods, places of employment, civic organizations, or social clubs with which they may be associated, using phone books and the Internet as mentioned previously. The extra step of doing this advance homework pays big dividends, because it increases the likelihood of a referral and removes the blank stares that oftentimes accompany an open-ended referral request.

This idea has led to several questions from readers, so we thought it might be helpful to spend more time on this topic, in a Q&A format.

Question 1: How do you define the term "advocate?"

An advocate is a person or group of people who have an almost inexplicable desire to see you and your practice succeed – they're promoters, campaigners, and supporters of your business. In addition to clients, advocates can be personal acquaintances, family members, prospects, and other professionals. Think about your practice – do you know someone who goes out of their way to give you referrals or to introduce you to new people? They are your advocates.

Question 2: I don't receive enough referrals. Will advocacy help?

One of the biggest benefits to regularly promoting advocacy in your practice is an increase in referrals. In addition to increased referrals, advisors who use advocacy techniques tend to receive references that are more qualified and ready to do business. It is truly a technique for finding new clients who look like your best clients.

Question 3: I would feel more comfortable talking in person with my clients about advocacy – would client meetings be as effective as a telephone campaign?

Yes. In fact, some of the most successful advocacy campaigns we've seen have been a series of one-on-one client meetings. Whether they're meetings specifically arranged to discuss advocacy or adding advocacy as a topic in a regular client review meeting, the process works well, as long as there's an agenda and all the steps (see question 4) are followed. Schedule one "advocacy lunch" per week for the next 60 days – your results will be measurable.

Question 4: An advocacy call to my clients sounds like a good idea. Can you elaborate on the steps?

Step 1: Create a simple list of your possible advocates. Start with your clients and add other people you believe would be good sources of referrals, such as prospects, professionals, or personal acquaintances.

Step 2: Refine your understanding of the uniqueness and commonalities of those people you've identified as potential advocates. Your goal is to develop resources for lists of potential referrals. Ask yourself a few questions: To which civic or social groups do your advocates belong? Which companies or industry groups? Are they on boards of charities or local corporations? Simply record several of these characteristics for each potential advocate on your list.

Step 3: Using your research from Step 2, prepare a list of two to five promising referrals for each person you intend to call or meet. This will mean spending time surfing the Internet, reviewing telephone books, or researching club directories and annual reports. The more time you spend, the more successful you'll be. Creativity is a must.

Step 4: Get together with your advocates and leverage your knowledge. This means talking with each one about the importance of advocacy and the work you've done in anticipation of your call or meeting. Go through your referral list, one at a time, and ask for feedback. For each reference, request permission to use your advocate's name when you make your initial contact.

Step 5: Finally, meet with your references. Set the stage by reviewing your unique value proposition (UVP) and your approach to advocacy. Your referrals need to understand your approach to both managing (UVP) and growing (advocacy) your business. You'll stand out from the crowd as a true professional.

Question 5: Does this process really work?

One of the most significant success stories we've seen occurred late last year, for an advisor who learned our advocacy process. The advisor decided on a 90-day referral-gathering cycle. He did all his research during the first 30 days (Steps 1, 2 and 3), held client meetings during the next 30 days (step 4) and spent the final month meeting with his referrals (step 5). Over the first complete cycle, this advisor was able to increase his assets under management from $50 million to $75 million – a 50% increase – just by applying our advocacy process to his practice.

Question 6: How do I learn more about building advocacy and beginning my own campaign?

A great way to become even more familiar with this topic is our CD-ROM, *Building Advocacy: How to Find More Clients Who Look like Your*

Best Clients. The CD contains an audio and visual presentation with complete details on each of the five advocacy steps, plus worksheets for starting your own campaign.

Appendix 1
Client Letters and Client Profile Form

Dear *<personalize>*,

Making the Most Of the Next Financial Year

As we begin the New Year, we feel it's important to spend time with each of our clients. In conducting reviews this year, we have 4 objectives:

1. Evaluate our progress in the current financial year
2. Review and clarify your financial goals
3. Discuss new tax, IRA, and retirement planning considerations
4. Set priorities for the next financial year

With this in mind, please complete as much of the enclosed wealth profile as possible and return it in the enclosed return envelope. Once we receive your information, we'll call to set up a time to get together. Our meeting will be a time to fill in any missing information, answer questions you may have, and set direction for the next 12 months.

Financial needs can change frequently. The information obtained from this profile and meeting will help maximize our understanding of your financial aspirations and it will help us to continue providing you with the best possible service and advice.

Sincerely:

<your name>

P.S. Please don't let the profile overwhelm you. Though it may seem lengthy, it's one way we can be certain you receive the type of service you deserve. We can always finish it when we meet.

Client Letter Two

Dear (personalize)

Setting the Stage for the Next Financial Year

Welcome to *<the next financial year>*! We cannot thank you enough for your past business, loyalty and camaraderie. We look forward to another year of providing you with the highest levels of service and advice. You truly make our work worthwhile and pleasurable.

As we consider the challenges and opportunities which lie ahead in the New Year, there are several key considerations worth reviewing. From both "big picture" and individual client perspectives, we see much more reason for optimism than pessimism. The resiliency of our country and economy, combined with disciplined personal planning, will almost always lead to positive results.

The Big Picture

Though we don't profess to be economists or political scientists, there are three "big picture" issues to which we're paying the most attention – Interest Rates, Tax Law Changes, and Global Turbulence. These topics have the potential to sweep the headlines and sway the overall economic landscape, so let's take a brief look at each one:

Interest Rates – Whether you're considering your investment or loan portfolio, it's almost impossible to ignore the activities of the Federal Reserve. Interest rate increases raise borrowing costs and cause many investors to reconsider their asset allocations.

Tax Law Changes are even more unpredictable than interest rates. The discourse in Washington makes it difficult to know which priorities will be addressed. On balance, there seems to be a movement towards simplification. And – though any change would have both supporters and detractors – any adjustment that will reduce confusion and encourage investment is always welcome.

Global Turbulence is perhaps the most sensitive issue to address in this type of letter. Discussion of war, terrorism, and loss of life evoke emotions that are not easily satisfied. At the same time – barring the unexpected – we're hopeful the worst is behind us. If the next financial year is a year in which our brave soldiers begin to return home, we should see a boost in overall morale as well as in the financial markets.

Updating Your Plans and Priorities

No matter the direction of any of these "big picture" issues, it's important we stay focused on your personal plans and priorities. Though it's nice to have the wind in our sails, it's always better to have a sturdy ship with a logical destination. To be sure we get the New Year off to a successful start, we'll soon be contacting you, to review your financial plan in-person. In conducting our first quarter client meetings, we have 3 objectives:

Evaluate your progress and clarify your goals

First, we'll take a look back at the current financial year and determine how much progress we've made toward your long-term objectives. We also want to be sure we clarify our understanding of your goals and identify any new ones. This will help ensure that your asset allocation, retirement income projections, and estate plans are up-to-date.

Discuss your tax, IRA and retirement planning options

These planning considerations are often complicated by modifications in tax laws and regulations. There have been a number of changes over the past year. We want to work with you and with your tax advisor, to be sure we understand your individual concerns and considerations.

Feedback and advocacy

Finally, we want to ask for your feedback on our work and share our philosophy on advocacy. Your opinion of how we're doing is important as we continuously strive to improve our services. Advocacy allows us to add new clients to our business through careful selection and client referrals. This conservative approach allows us to control our growth and maintain our commitments to service.

Closing Option One – Include Profile:

The Next Financial Year Wealth Profile Update

We've enclosed a copy of our survey, "The Next Financial Year Wealth Profile Update." Please take some time to complete as much as possible and then return it to us in the enclosed envelope. Don't worry if you need to leave some blank spaces. Once we receive your information, we'll call you to set up a time to get together. Our meeting will be a time to fill in any missing information, answer questions you may have, and set direction for the next 12 months.

Thank you for taking time to read this rather lengthy letter and filling in the update form. We know this may seem like a big undertaking, but we also know this review will allow us to continue working with you, to achieve your investment and financial objectives.

All the best,

<your name>

P.S. Please don't let the profile overwhelm you. Though it may seem lengthy, it's one way we can be certain you receive the type of service you deserve. We can always finish it when we meet.

Closing Option Two – Profile *Not* Included:

Thank you for taking time to read this rather lengthy letter. We hope it offered some valuable perspective for the year ahead. Also, please expect a call from our office over the next couple weeks, to arrange a mutually convenient time for our review meeting. If you have pressing issues you need to discuss and would like to meet with us sooner, simply give us a call and we'll be happy to make our meeting even more of a priority.

All the best,

<your name>

Client Profile Questionnaire

Long Version:

Preferred Client Questionnaire

Thank you for taking the time to begin completing this update.

Feel free to use the back of these pages or extra paper if necessary.

1. Do we need to update your personal information?

Name(s)

Address

Home Phone

Business Phone

Cell Phone

Personal email address

Business email address

Which email address should we use to contact you with important updates?

2. Have there been any changes to your employment related information?

Employer	Spouse employer
Current position	Spouse current position
Annual income (salary, bonus, other)	Spouse income

Do you have a company sponsored retirement plan(s)? Indicate **self or spouse** plan.

- Type (Pension, 401-k, deferred compensation, other):

- Value:

- Would you like us to review this plan **(yes or no)**?

- Have you set/changed your retirement date **(yes or no)**? Please list:

3. How are we doing?

On a scale of 1 to 5, with 1 meaning needs improvement and 5 meaning we are meeting your expectations, how would you rate us on the following categories?

_____ Service, responsiveness to your inquiries
- Are you aware of any outstanding service issues?

_____ Communication, frequency of contact
- Should we be in more, less or about the same amount of contact?

_____ Planning and investment Advice, properly understand your goals

Please use the space below to indicate areas where you see need for **improvement**.

Please use the space below to list what you believe to be **our strengths**.

4. Financial and Investment Goals and Objectives

What is your primary financial goal?

What other objectives do you have (list all)?

Have your investment objectives changed over the past year **(yes or no)**? Why?

Have the timelines changed for any of your objectives?

Do you consider yourself to be an **aggressive, moderate or conservative** investor?

What **percent of your investments** should be dedicated to **growth** and what percent should be allocated to **income**?

5. Risk concerns and interest rates

As it relates to investment volatility, would you say you feel differently today than you did at the beginning of *<previous year>*?

If the stock market were to experience a year of double digit losses, would you expect your current overall portfolio to perform **better, the same, or worse** than the market?

If the stock market were to experience a year of double digit gains, would you expect your current overall portfolio to perform **better, the same, or worse** than the market?

Do you believe interest rates are heading **higher or lower**?

Do you expect the direction of interest rates to affect your current asset allocation – stocks, bonds, cash, and alternative investments?

Do you expect the direction of interest rates to affect your loan portfolio?

6. Longer-term planning

What does long term mean to you? How many years out is long term?

Have you updated your **wills, trusts, life insurance policies, or other estate planning** tools during the past year? If so, which ones?

Have you begun or are you considering planning for any **new financial goals** – (goals like retirement planning, education planning or charitable giving)?

Do you hold any retirement, investment, or savings accounts which we may not be aware of and on which you would like a second opinion? If yes, please **list below:**

There have been several tax law changes relating to IRA contribution limits, Roth IRAs, rollover considerations and minimum required distributions. Should we spend time reviewing your IRAs, rollover accounts and company sponsored retirement plans? **Please list** any specific concerns or considerations:

Do you have any income tax concerns **(yes or no)**? **Please describe:**

7. What other professionals are involved on your personal, financial, and investment planning?

Attorney (name and phone number)

Accountant (name and phone number)

Other (responsibility, name and phone number)

8. We will list "key findings" during our review meeting.

1. _____

2. _____

3. _____

4. _____

5. _____

9. We may request additional documentation during our review meeting.

1. _____

2. _____

3. _____

10. Our business grows only through the careful selection of new clients and referrals from our clients. Please let us know if you would like to make an introduction.

_____

_____

Short Version:

Preferred Client Questionnaire

Thank you for taking the time to begin completing this questionnaire; we will address more specific questions during our next appointment. Feel free to use the back of these pages or extra paper if necessary.

Section 1: General Updates

1. Do we need to update any of your **personal information** such as addresses or phone numbers **(Circle: yes or no)?** If yes, please list changes here:

2. We like to send important ideas and updates via email, **please list (or update) your email address below.** We'll never share your email address with anyone else.

3. Have there been any changes to your **employment related information** (name of employer, promotions, bonuses or major salary increases) **(Circle: yes or no)?** Describe below:

4. Do you (or your spouse) have a company sponsored **retirement plan(s)? (Circle: yes or no)** Please list type (pension, 401-k, deferred compensation, other) and current value. Would you like us to review this plan(s) **(Circle: yes or no)?**

Section 2: Personal, financial and investment goals

1. Have your personal, financial, or investment goals changed over the past year **(Circle: yes or no)?** If so, please give a brief explanation:

2. Have the timelines changed for any of your goals **(Circle: yes or no)?** If so, please give a brief explanation:

3. Have you updated your wills, trusts, life insurance policies, or other estate planning tools during the past year **(Circle: yes or no)?** If so, which ones?

4. Have you begun or are you considering planning for any new financial goals – (goals like retirement planning, education planning or charitable giving) **(Circle: yes or no)?**

5. Do you hold any retirement, investment, or savings accounts which we may not be aware of and on which you would like a second opinion **(Circle: yes or no)?** If yes, please **list below:**

6. Will you have any special income tax concerns in <*next financial year*> **(Circle: yes or no)?** Please describe:

Section 3: Key Findings (for use during our follow-up meeting)

1. _____
2. _____
3. _____

4: Referrals and references

Our business grows only through the careful selection of new clients and referrals from our important clients like. Please let us know if you would like to make any introductions.

1. _____
2. _____

Thanks for taking the time to complete this questionnaire. We appreciate your business and your loyalty.

Follow-up letter

<client name>
<client address>

Dear (personalize),

Wealth Profile Key Findings

Thank you for taking the time to meet with me, to discuss your *<next financial year>* Wealth Profile Update. The information we reviewed will allow us to continue providing you with the service and advice you need and to help you meet your financial goals. To summarize our meeting, below is a list of the Key Findings we uncovered during our discussion. I'll be following up on each of these items, as appropriate.

Key Findings:

1. _____

2. _____

3. _____

To help complete my work on these Key Findings, I'll need the following additional information. My assistant will call you, to see if *<he/she>* can assist you in pulling this documentation together.

Documentation needs:

1. _____

2. _____

3. _____

Again, thank you for your time; we'll work hard to use your profile update and our Key Findings to continue helping you work towards your financial goals.

Sincerely,

<your name>

Made in the USA
Lexington, KY
17 May 2019